THE

OPPOSITE

OF

HOLLYWOOD

For Curtis—
Thank you for all the
beautiful art you put out
there in ~ ~rld.

Marzo
SFCA 10/2015

D1529269

ALSO BY MARGO PERIN

*How I Learned to Cook & Other Writings
on Complex Mother-Daughter Relationships*

Only the Dead Can Kill: Stories from Jail

Spiral of Gratitude Memorial Poem

THE
OPPOSITE
OF
HOLLYWOOD

an autobiographical novel

MARGO PERIN

WHOA NELLY PRESS

Copyright © 2014 by Margo Perin

All rights reserved. No part of this publication may be reproduced, distributed,
or transmitted in any form or by any means, including photocopying, recording,
or other electronic or mechanical methods, without the prior written permission
of the publisher, except in the case of brief quotations embodied in critical
reviews and certain other noncommercial uses permitted by copyright law.
For permission requests, write to the publisher, addressed
"Attention: Permissions Coordinator," at the address below.

Whoa Nelly Press
3442 Sacramento Street
San Francisco, CA 94118
whoanellypress.com

Ordering information:
Quantity sales. Special discounts are available on quantity purchases by corporations,
associations, and others. For details, contact the publisher at the address above.
Orders by U. S. trade bookstores and wholesalers. Please contact the publisher.

Printed in the United States of America

Publisher's Cataloging-in-Publication data

Perin, Margo
The Opposite of Hollywood: an autobiographical novel / Margo Perin.
ISBN 978-0-692-31564-4
1. Perin, Margo. 2. Perin, Margo — Fiction. 3. Novel — autobiographical.
2. Children of criminals — daughter 3. Exile — United States,
United Kingdom, Bahamas, Mexico

FIRST EDITION

Book Design by Gretchen Achilles

For Marci Klane, for more than I can say,

Valerie Mejer Caso, who provided the oars,

and especially for all the Toscas of the world.

CHAPTER ONE

HOME

When I was a child, my father changed our name six times, once for every time we left town. That was so he could hide from people looking for him. Our first names remained the same—this was my mother's department. She liked the movies and named us after movie stars, except for a brief spell when she switched to opera and named me Tosca and my next brother down Figaro.

There were seven of us in all. First there was Ava, then Natalie, Kirk, me and Figaro, and Rock. The same doctor delivered all of us at New York General Hospital, and after Rock was born, he made my mother promise not to have any more because it was dangerous. She had been having kids one after the other, and her body was all stretched out of shape. But my father wanted her pregnant—"He liked me like that," she said—and three years later, when I was seven, Marilyn came as the finale to my mother's motherhood.

The first time we moved I was four. It was a few blocks away and several rungs up the ladder in New York City, but my name stayed the same—Tosca Ring. There were only six of us then. I came home from nursery school on the school bus and found everyone gone. As I opened our door on the third floor of the tenement building, all I saw was the fat back of a strange man. He was staring out the kitchen window. His white shirtsleeves were rolled up, revealing hairy elbows. The cracked wooden stool he sat on was the only piece of furniture left in the empty brown rooms.

I ran back downstairs, sure he was the man my mother had warned me about who would tempt little girls up to his apartment by offering them candy, tell them to look out the window, and then shoot them. I stood on the street screaming until someone came to help me. It was Wally, my father's friend. His thick arms swung low as he bent down. He had been upstairs, waiting to take me to our new apartment.

"Didn't Mommy tell you about moving today?" he asked, wiping his hands with a rolled-up handkerchief. "What's the matter? Didn't you know that was me up there?" It was the beginning of summer, and sweat rolled off his fat red cheeks.

I stared at him wordlessly.

Wally put away his handkerchief. "I guess Mommy forgot to tell you," he said.

The new building was on York and Sixty-First and had a black-and-white-striped canopy at the entrance. We rode up to the twenty-first floor in an elevator, to the penthouse suite. My father greeted Wally warmly as I headed around the L-shaped corner behind the front door. I ran into Kirk whooping and sliding in his socks along the wooden floor. I threw off my shoes and joined him, shouting gleefully as I slid faster and faster back and forth across our new living room. Then I lost my balance and fell hard on my arm.

"Ow!" I cried.

My mother appeared looking frazzled and called to my father in an annoyed voice, "Take her to the hospital. She might have broken her arm."

At the hospital, my father joked with the doctor, whose name was Dr. Carpenter. They chatted in a friendly way while the doctor wrapped a plaster cast around my arm. Smiling cheerfully at me, he said, "Now you can get everyone to give you their autograph!"

When my father and I got back to the apartment, everything had turned purple. There were purple drapes, purple rugs scattered on the glassy parqueted floors that we now had a maid to sweep and polish, and a purple U-shaped couch that made the back of my legs itch when I waited for my father to come home and hold a conference. Bunches of glass grapes and plums fashioned into a heavy chandelier hung over a mahogany dining table. The walls were covered with framed Renoir and Degas reproductions. They had flecks of pink to match the purple.

At first, there was a chrome and glass table at the edge of the living room, but my mother stood on it one day to change a lightbulb and it broke, sending shards of glass and blood all over the rugs. Her hands shook like dry leaves as she screamed at the maid to clean it up. I don't remember which maid it was.

Owing to my mother's temper, they came and went quicker than the seasons.

We lived in the penthouse suite on York Avenue for three years, from when I was four to seven. That was before we started throwing away countries and cities like old candy wrappers. At the back of the apartment was one bedroom for the boys and another for the girls. My parents slept at the front and had their own bathroom, which we were forbidden to enter. When they went out, I used to sneak in and try on their things, including white napkins from a plain cardboard box balanced on the back of the toilet tank. My sister Natalie crept in with me once and told me the cotton was special toilet paper that only women could use. I tried to add a pad when my brothers and I stuffed toilet paper breasts under our tee shirts, but it was too bulky and I had to tear it up into small wads and flush it down the toilet before my mother got back. One of the maids, Eileen I think, discovered that the toilet was all clogged up and started yelling. She was Irish and took me to visit her family in Brooklyn, probably to show me what a normal family looked like. They sat in the living room with its worn brown carpet and watched TV as they ate thick hamburgers in soft white buns and passed salt and pepper during the commercials.

In our new apartment, everything was different from before. It wasn't homey like the old place. There we had been crammed into four small rooms and a poky kitchen overlooking a courtyard filled with garbage cans and squabbling children. We had played with other kids who lived in the building while my mother watched us from upstairs and made peanut butter and jelly sandwiches for lunch. We screamed and shouted, ducking to avoid the bucket of cold water doused on us when the old woman upstairs had enough of us yelling "Witch!" at her. My father used to be home more, changing the babies' diapers in the living room where there was always the faint smell of urine and sour milk.

Now we had room, what my mother called a view—and one another. I wasn't allowed to play with my best friend, Cynthia, anymore from the old tenement, not since we'd moved. I'd gone over there once and her mother had yelled at me for asking why they didn't have a seat on their toilet. She had gone bright red. Her teeth were uneven and yellow.

"Not everyone can afford one!" she shouted. "Just 'cause your father all of a sudden has money doesn't mean you can come over here and be a snob!"

"What do you need Cynthia for?" asked my mother after I cried all the way back home. "You have all your brothers and sisters to play with."

So I played on the high balcony overlooking York Avenue with my brothers, or Natalie when she would let me, to the muffled roar of cars honking and trucks screeching as they crossed over the Fifty-Ninth Street Bridge into Queens. Sometimes I was allowed to go alone to the playground across the street and I would sit on the swings, watching cars creep over the bridge, wondering how many it would take to collapse and fall on top of me.

———

We moved to York Avenue because my father had started his own business. What kind of business I didn't know. He hurried to and from work, hardly stopping to give my mother a quick peck on the cheek. In the morning, we were forbidden to talk to him before he'd had his first cup of coffee. He'd shuffle into the kitchen early while we were still sleeping and brew it up. Then he would pour it from cup to cup so it wouldn't burn his lips. He never ate in the morning, just slurped the coffee. After we were all awake and sitting at the table, my mother tiptoed around, serving us soft-boiled eggs in blue and white bowls filled with Saltines. We were too scared to make a sound and I spooned my food quietly, with my eyes on my father.

His hands were shiny and smooth, almost waxy, and if he was in a good mood, he would stroke one of our heads as he moved to the percolator. But he didn't usually do that unless he'd poured liquid from a bottle under the sink and had a sip or two first. He didn't always drink from this bottle, just when there were dark brown circles under his eyes. After finishing his coffee, he would shuffle out again and that would be the last I saw of him until the next morning. Unless my mother kept us up for his return at night so he could hold a family conference. Then, when the blinds were down and the lights blazing, he seemed like another person. Instead of the man who slouched over his cup in the morning, hair rumpled, eyes baggy and creased, this one was dressed in a crisp suit and tie and had slicked-back hair and a hard face and hands. I didn't know which one I feared more.

Early in life, my father came to the decision that he would be different from other people: better than, more than. That meant his life was going to be different from everyone else's, more exciting, harder to define. He started lying early on. He was the youngest of six boys in a family of Russian immigrants, but he said his parents were French. He was Jewish but said he was from a line of French Huguenots. It embarrassed him that his father was a bus conductor and his mother a domestic and spoke only Yiddish, so he took elocution classes and pretended he was a Columbia University graduate. And the only way I knew this was from his brother's wife Judith whom I met long after I'd left my family.

But one thing my father always told the truth about was when he tried to move to Russia. Over the years, he told each of us in turn, slapping the side of his chair for emphasis.

"I joined the Communist Party when I was seventeen. They were fools. I saw it right away. They didn't know anything about Communism. Only I knew what was really going on. So after the war, when I'd saved enough money—Mommy and I were married then and Ava only a few months old—we sold everything and left. I thought we were going for good. But those idiots! They thought we were spies! They wouldn't even let us in the country!"

He laughed bitterly. "So, we tried again, this time from

Czechoslovakia. You know what those imbeciles did then? They kept us under house arrest until they deported us back. Mommy couldn't even go out for food for the baby. For five whole weeks."

"What did you do then, Daddy?" I asked.

He snorted. "Made money." He didn't mention how his mother must have felt, having fled pogroms, that her son was trying to move back to Russia.

Outnumbered seven to two, my parents forgot all about Communism and ran the family along the lines of divide and conquer. They set the rules and relied on us to tell on one another. High up on this unwritten constitution was the rule No Sugar Allowed. Part of the reason my father gave us paltry weekly allowances was so we couldn't buy candy—the other was so we would know the value of money. Natalie and I partook in a counterinsurgency plan and went on stealing sprees in candy stores.

My mother depended on us to tell on one another to control us better. She called it "help with the kids." She would add up our misdeeds and have us silently lined up on the purple couch in time for my father's arrival at the dark end of the day.

"He's going to kill you," she'd say gleefully. "Just wait until he calls a conference as s-oo-oo-n as he walks in that door!" Before he had his coat off, she would cry, "You wouldn't believe what I had to put up with today!"

I squirmed on the itchy fabric of the couch and watched my father slowly remove his overcoat—cashmere in winter, linen in summer—and stride to the middle of the open-plan living room in measured steps. As he came closer his short figure grew in height so that he loomed over us. He hitched up his tailored trousers so they wouldn't ruffle and sat down in the matching purple armchair. The aroma of liquor, Old Spice, and cigarette smoke filled the room until I felt like I was choking. My mother leaned against the wall with a smile of satisfaction as the proceedings began.

"Ava," my father would begin, his waxy, manicured hands playing teasingly with each other. He always began with the eldest and worked his way down. "What were you doing at four o'clock when you should have been home?"

His words came slowly, and he paused to suck the space between his teeth with a faint hissing noise. He spoke deliberately, at half speed. His pauses were sometimes so long that his face would retreat into the wallpaper.

"I was in the library doing my homework," said Ava. She hid behind a wall of hair as she bit her short pink fingernails.

"Oh you were, were you?"

My father crossed his legs carefully so he wouldn't crease his pants. He pulled out a bright white handkerchief from his breast pocket where it was folded into a triangle and blew his nose. Then he placed it back carefully so that, too, wouldn't crease.

"Mommy tells me you went to someone's house. Didn't I warn you not to go anywhere without permission?" He pulled out an unfiltered Pall Mall from a flat gold cigarette case and tapped it slowly.

Ava kept her eyes to the floor.

"Look at me while I'm talking!"

I squeezed Natalie's hand tighter, hoping she wouldn't pee herself again. Natalie always peed herself when Ava got hit. My father grunted and reached under the chair for the ping-pong paddle.

"Come here," he said, balancing his cigarette on a jagged crystal ashtray.

Ava stood up and obediently pulled down her bottoms, porcelain skin shining as she lay across his lap. Everything looked as if it were in slow motion, my father's hand floating down, paddle held high, the hard slap on my sister's buttocks, her sudden jolt, sweat pouring down my father's nose. My heart stopped as I watched the large beauty mark frozen on my sister's thigh move up and down with each slap.

Natalie's knuckles turned white from clenching them so tightly, but she couldn't stop herself from crying, "Please, Daddy, don't hit her! Don't hit her anymore. Please, Daddy!"

"Get over here!" my father yelled, pushing Ava off his lap. "How dare you interfere?"

It didn't matter anymore that Natalie was supposed to be punished for not setting the table when my mother had told her to. Now she was in trouble for sticking up for Ava.

After Kirk it was my turn.

"Are you calling your mother a liar for denying you were eating chocolate?" he shouted. "How dare you!"

As I lay straddled across my father's knee, the hot slap of the paddle stung my bare buttocks. My father wouldn't let us cushion the blows with even the thinnest cotton of our underwear.

When my father had finished with the youngest, except for Rock, who was still too young to be held over his knee, we would be sent to bed with strict orders not to speak.

The conferences started with our move up the income ladder and continued until we had to leave New York. They became a weekly event, but no matter how many times they happened, I never got used to my father forcing us over his knee and thrashing us. I didn't know if he grew scared or just preoccupied with other things, but the last conference we had was before we left for Mexico and Ava, who was now eleven and developing, refused to pull up her slip and bend over my father's knee. Nothing he did could make her until finally he lunged over and tried to slap her on the head. He missed, and his hand landed on her lower lip, splitting it. Forever after, a thick scar ran down the middle of my sister's mouth.

I thought that I could be different from the others if only I could figure out something about him that the rest didn't know. I thought maybe if I acted as he did, copied what he did, he wouldn't hit me. So I examined him, recording his movements. I nodded while I ate, as he did, picked my teeth after sucking on the last of my food, and smoothed back my wavy hair from my forehead when he was between saying things at the supper table. One night at dinner, I kept quiet, observing carefully as he told us about someone he knew. He held his thumb and forefinger to his head and pretended to shoot himself. "What a nutcase! What a fruit!" He laughed, turning over his red meat with a gleaming silver fork. He always rubbed his silverware clean before putting it into his mouth.

"Ha-ha!" I laughed along, holding my belly as if it were the funniest thing I'd ever heard. Meanwhile, I searched my brains to think of a story to match his.

"Yeah, Daddy! My teacher's a nut, too!" I said, holding my finger and thumb to my head at the same angle he had, throwing my head back as he had. Everyone else kept their heads down, eating.

There was a long silence. My father's face turned dark. "Don't you *ever* do that again," he yelled, eyes flashing from narrowed slits. "You have to respect your teachers! You do that again and you'll be sorry!"

Stunned, my head snapped down. Natalie patted my hand under the table, but there was nothing she could do. There was nothing anyone could do.

My parents strove to adjust our lifestyle to fit our new circumstances. Piano was the instrument of social betterment and so they hired Mr. Oldstein to teach us to play—a half hour each, two children a day. Mr. Oldstein was small and dry and had a bristly stubble on his face that seemed like it was covered in white dust. He spoke with a German accent.

"No, ve do not play ze piano mit die elbows; du muss play mit die fingers!"

He always wore the same suit—gray with flecks of white on his stooped shoulders—and he looked far off into the distance as if watching a bird fly around the room when he played fragments of Mozart and Chopin. He sounded and even smelled a little like my grandmother—musty, as if he lived in a closet— but, unlike my grandmother, he was always angry. When my fingers strayed to the wrong notes, he slammed his small fists down on the keys and bit my pinky so I would hurt as much as he did.

The best part of the lesson was when Mr. Oldstein had had enough of my clumsy hammering and threw my hands aside. He spread his stubby fingers and danced them up and down the black and white keys, swaying from side to side as he took off to another world, perhaps the one from where he had fled during the Second World War.

"They killed all my family," he told me once, unraveling a worn handkerchief from his trouser pocket to wipe his eyes. "My mother, my father, my sister. So I came to America and now I play the piano."

I didn't understand what he said although it sounded like my grandmother when she talked about Russia, before my mother kicked her out for feeding us chocolate raisins behind her back. So I just kept quiet, scrutinizing his face for how I should feel about what he said. Sometimes I cried with him, but mostly I just sat and watched in silence.

M y parents went out almost every night, either to an opera or a movie. They put Ava in charge, shut off the hallway light, and locked the front door behind them. One night, after my piano lesson, I sat on my mother's twin bed and watched her get ready to go. Kirk was having his lesson in the living room—"No, it goes like this!" crescendoed through the closed door, followed by Kirk's loud cry. Mr. Oldstein must have bit him, too.

My mother didn't seem to notice and strutted between the walk-in closet and her purple vanity table with its three mirrors so she could see herself from all sides, trying on first a slinky black skirt, then a loose blue one, and finally settling on a dress with large imprinted tulips and waving green grass that stretched tightly across her bosom. She took it off again to powder herself, once under the armpits, twice behind the knees. She hummed as she dressed, "La-la-la-de-da," like she'd gone somewhere else. She reached for a pair of silk stockings and plopped down on the bed. I rolled over just before she sat on me.

"What the heck—" she gasped, clutching the stockings to her breasts. She frowned and said angrily, "What are you doing here?" She turned back to her vanity table and drew black lines on her eyebrows.

After my last lesson, she'd put me in the bath, leaving me alone while I splashed around waiting for her to come back. As the water turned icy, I stood up and yelled for her. When she didn't come, I yelled at the top of my lungs. The door burst open and Mr. Oldstein landed in the room.

"Vot's wrong," he yelled, waving his arms. "You are okay?"

I gaped at him, suffused in embarrassment that my teacher was seeing me naked.

"I want my mother," I whimpered, clutching my arms around me.

"It's all right, don't vorry, you be okay. I get your mama." As he left the room, he mumbled to himself, "Dese crazy people, leaving a child in ze bath like that."

My sisters and I didn't have dolls, not since my mother had bought one for Ava when she was three. Natalie had been only one and a half and had pulled off its arms and legs. My mother didn't see any point in them after that.

Natalie was three years older than I, and she dressed up in an old pink bedspread in the room we shared to perform the operas that my mother blasted on the radio in the other room.

"Carmen! C-a-r-m-e-n!" she trilled as she swept along the pale green carpet from one end of the bedroom to the other, her gown trailing behind her in lumpy folds. Freckles crossed her face and arms like spattered paint.

"Carmen," I croaked in a higher voice, tripping on the bed-spread in her wake.

Natalie turned around, petulant. "That's my part," she frowned. She placed the train in my hands. "Keep your mouth shut and just follow."

"But I want to sing!" I cried.

Natalie was direct. "If you want to stay here, you have to do what I say."

Without another word, I picked up the train.

One Indian summer afternoon, I sat on the bedroom carpet riveted to a *National Geographic* magazine, splashed with photographs of naked women with breasts protruding like chocolate ice cream cones. Natalie blew in and kneeled on my bed situated under the wide sliding-glass window.

"Hey, look at that!" she said.

I looked up, reluctant to tear myself away from the pictures. "What?"

"Whew!" Natalie whistled. Three pigtails hung crookedly from her head. She did her hair by herself and wouldn't let anyone touch it. "Just look at that!"

My curiosity aroused, I edged toward the window. "What?"

The faint scent of bananas wafted under my nose; Natalie always smelled like that.

She pointed and said, "Look, there's the moon! Can't you see it?"

I clambered onto the bed. "Where?"

"Over there! Look!"

Distracted by the flashing red, white, and blue of the Pepsi

Cola sign on the other side of the East River, I searched frantically to see what she saw.

"Where is it?" Maybe she wouldn't let me play with her anymore. I banged my fist on the windowsill. "Come on, Natalie,
where is it?"

I turned around. The room was empty. And my magazine
was no longer on the floor where I'd left it.

It wasn't all one way. At the concrete square of playground,
it took me a minute to register that Natalie was hanging off her
end of the seesaw by the shorts while I sat at the bottom.

"Help, I'm stuck!" she screamed.

I started to rise to my feet. "I'll go get Mommy!"

"No!" she bellowed. "Don't move! Whatever you do, don't
get up!"

But it was too late. Luckily, Natalie landed on her arms, not
her head, and arrived home with only cuts and bruises. We told
my mother that someone pushed her off the slide.

My mother's closet smelled like her, a musky blend of roses and powder, mixed with a sharper, fruity smell that
was sometimes on her breath when she kissed us good night.
Her fingers were long and skinny, and they stung like winter
branches against my cheek when she was mad. "I should have
been a piano player," she would laugh, reclining against the
purple loveseat as she touched up her nails, which were always

chipped at the top. She said it was because of the kids, but I thought it was because she was always breaking them on the windows. "It's so hot," she would yell, slamming up the windows so hard they shook. On her cheeks she smudged red circles and drew thick black lines around her eyes and blue patches above and below. Her lip color changed with each outfit. As she got older, the lipstick got higher. The last time I saw her, her upper lip almost reached her nose.

In the heat of New York summers, my mother went up to the roof, way above cars squealing and people propelling along the street far below. She sat back in a stringy plastic chair next to the other housewives and on her chest balanced an aluminum shield the shape of her vanity table mirrors. She never said much to the other women. She just sat with her eyes closed, face to the sun, a slight smile on her lips, her toes twitching, her thoughts a million miles away.

"Dad was in the merchant marines during the war," she told me once, evoking the photograph of her with ivory skin and long black hair curling down her back in our family album. "I met him when he was on leave." She sighed. "He asked me to marry him after two weeks. I told him I had to think about it." She laughed her small nervous laugh, tossing her head coquettishly. "I thought he was a little weird, but he was so gorgeous." She sat quietly, gazing into the distance.

"He was over the moon when I said yes. You should have seen how happy he was. He even introduced me to his family.

They were a bunch of snobs," she added as an aside, her eyes flashing in anger. "They never approved of me."

Her mouth twisted with resentment. "After I said yes he went back to sea, and then you know what he did? I went to meet him at the docks on his next leave and he told me he'd changed his mind. Right in front of his family. I felt like such an idiot, him embarrassing me like that. It took him a year to finally make up his mind."

"How old were you?" I asked, thinking she wouldn't notice if I slipped it in quick enough.

She pursed her lips, turning her face from me. "Don't start that again!"

Like my father, my mother barely talked about the past. She said she was from an Italian-English background and had three sisters; her father was an English parson, she said, and her mother an Italian opera singer. She was vague about what part of Italy her mother was from.

When my mother was ten, she said, their father "had a fight with the landlord and threw a bag of groceries at him." A social worker turned up at her school and placed her and her sisters in an orphanage and then fostered them out. My mother didn't reveal that my grandmother had tried to kill herself several times, sometimes in front of my mother and her sisters, and eventually succeeded, or that my grandfather was out of work and died a few years later. Both grandparents were Hungarian Jewish immigrants who couldn't make a go of it in the new country. But she would, and that meant leaving who she was behind.

On one rainy afternoon my mother sat with her feet up on the table in an orange and pink housecoat and read a libretto as Kirk and Fig and I played Thunder and Lightning under the piano. As always, her head was at an angle, as if dodging a sudden blow. Her dark hair fell over her ears, a shelter from our noise. Suddenly her head snapped up.

"Keep it down!" Her hands rustled through the white pages on her lap. "Can't you kids be quiet for a second?"

"Shut up, Tosca!" my older brother taunted, as if the noise were my fault. Kirk had the dark vibrancy of my mother's side of the family. He looked just like Ava—short black curly hair, red cheeks in ivory skin, and freckles bridging a straight nose. He often stood like my father, fully erect, arms and legs outstretched, with his chest puffed out like General Sherman at the entrance to Central Park.

"You shut up!" I retorted.

"Shut up, fatty!" squeaked Fig, his godlike power to create thunder and lightning forgotten. He was a pale chestnut color, like wet autumn leaves.

I turned around and swiped him. "Shut up, copycat!"

Kirk came to his rescue. "Cut it out, ugly!"

I pushed him. Then I ran, fast losing ground next to his swift, confident stride. I landed sidesaddle on the back of the couch. My brothers took up a game of tug-of-war with my legs.

"Ouch!" I screamed. "Lemme go!" A ball of heat and pain exploded in my groin.

"Ow! M-o-m-m-y!"

"What's the matter now?" she snapped, wrenching me by the arm.

A stream of blood leaked out of my shorts.

"I'm bleeding," I shrieked.

"You can't be!" she said, hauling me off to the small bathroom around the corner. She locked the door behind us and yanked down my shorts. Holding me at arm's length and pulling my lips apart, she squinted at my vagina, frowning. A look of repulsion spread over her face, like she was inspecting lettuce for bugs.

"Mommy, it hurts," I whimpered, looking down into the white line separating the two halves of her thick hair.

She shook her head with a familiar tsk. "Oh, that's nothing," she said briskly when she realized that I hadn't started my period. "Put your shorts back on."

When I was six-going-on-seven, I accompanied my mother to the grocery store. On the way back up to our apartment, as we waited by the elevator buttons, another woman who lived in the building joked about their fat stomachs. In surprise, I suddenly noticed the bulge protruding from my mother's middle.

The white of the neighbor's teeth flashed as she grinned, "This is my sixth. No matter what I do, I can't keep up with you. You're always one ahead!"

"Yeah," my mother nodded with a half smile. I always knew that when she didn't like somebody, her chin would thrust higher in the air. We bundled into the awaiting elevator.

"They're cute, but what a handful they turn out to be!" The woman chuckled and placed a friendly hand on my mother's arm.

My mother moved away, narrowing her eyes. I held my breath, waiting for a fight. It was like the time a red-faced woman had come up on the street and told her to stop hitting us with her handbag. Fig had to pee and cried because my mother made him do it between two cars and he didn't want anyone to see. When Kirk and I had tried to hide him, my mother's handbag came flying in our faces. She had screamed at the woman to mind her own business and dragged us away.

But now in the elevator, she merely smiled distantly at our neighbor, as if to remove herself from the conversation. "I really don't know what you mean," she said. A smudge of red lay outside the corner of her mouth—she'd chosen that color to match the purple and green chiffon scarf around her neck.

The woman looked surprised. I smiled at her so she wouldn't think my mother was rude. My mother caught me and frowned.

The elevator came to a standstill, stopping further conversation. "Well, take care," said the woman and the doors slid

THE OPPOSITE OF HOLLYWOOD

shut.

"Some people!" my mother bristled. She looked down at me. "I don't want you to talk to her. She's too nosy."

My mother disappeared for a few days and came home with Marilyn while I was still at school. When I ran into the apartment behind the others, there they stood by the dining room table, near the fruit chandelier, my mother holding this tiny thing in a fat white blanket. My brothers and sisters formed a circle to admire and hold her.

"Let me see!" I cried, hopping up and down with excitement, trying to peek around everyone to look. But no one noticed. They all stood around, clucking and laughing into the blanket, keeping it out of reach.

"Let me see!" I bellowed. At last, someone heard me and handed me the bundle. I peeked into my new sister's face. A layer of dark hair covered her cheeks, and her eyes sat in little wrinkles around screwed-up, puffy eyes. I looked up at my mother, mouth open and then, thwack! The baby's fist flew up into my jaw, smacking me with all her might. Everyone laughed while I bawled. My father took the baby back, admiring her strength.

I crept over to the couch and glared at everyone. None of them turned around to look.

After Marilyn arrived, my parents fought behind closed doors, thinking we couldn't hear them screaming insults at each other. Our conferences ceased for a while, and my father didn't show up for coffee in the morning. The fights seemed to be about money.

Natalie and I strayed farther away when we were allowed to roam free after school and on Saturday. I became absentminded and confused, knocking into furniture at home and losing my homework on the way to school. On the way home, playing Blind Man, Natalie and I held hands while one of us closed her eyes and was led by the other along the street. We dodged garbage cans, streetlights, and passersby, sometimes popping open our eyes to race across the street, sidestepping cars and trucks.

Natalie took first turn. As she was the older one, it was her right. Telling me to close my eyes, she led me carefully up the block and around the corner. Everything went black, and my ears filled with the roar of traffic as I inched my feet forward. The shrill of irregular car horns, screaming, sharp laughter, and the tap-tapping of high heels formed a thick wall around me. It reminded me of the night before, when I'd heard the sound of glass crashing against the wall and my mother hissing loudly, "Didn't you have any idea you might get caught?" My father's low tones had flowed like a dark river, with the letters FBI bobbing up every so often. This morning before school my mother, who always washed my father's socks and underwear by hand because he was allergic to detergent, had thrown a whole bowlful of black socks off the balcony. Later Kirk, Fig, and I copied her and added my father's felt hats, watching them sail through the air and land on people walking by. When Frank, the doorman, came up to complain, my mother told him to go to hell.

I opened my eyes. "Natalie, what does FBI mean?"

"Close your eyes, dummy. You're messing up the game."

"Okay," I said obediently and repeated, eyes closed, "What's FBI?"

"The really big police."

"How do you know?"

"I just know," she answered. She shook me impatiently. "Come on, let's switch."

"Okay." I grabbed her hand. "Close your eyes."

"Don't forget, Tosca, I can't see anything. You have to watch where you're going."

"I know! Come on, close your eyes."

Natalie looked scared. "Okay," she said. "I'm closing my eyes now."

I squeezed her hand and started walking. Women with large alligator handbags smiled as they passed me steering Natalie away from the wrought-iron railings lining the street. "Why are they coming to see Daddy?" I asked.

"Who?"

"The FBI." My father had been in a bad mood when he left this morning so I didn't think he wanted to see them, whoever they were.

"Ouch!"

My head turned. Bam! I had banged my sister into a streetlight, face first.

"Natalie!" I screamed at the blood gushing from her lip.

"Shut up! I'm all right," she said in a faraway voice, wiping her mouth with the back of her hand. Gingerly, she touched her front tooth. "I think I'm okay." Her face was completely white. She looked as she did when she had fallen out of a taxi as it swerved around Eighty-Sixth Street on the way back from the dentist. My mother hadn't noticed because we were all crushed into the back, and Natalie had almost gotten run over by a truck before my mother realized my screaming was not because Kirk pinched me but because something was wrong. Luckily, there was a traffic jam and nothing was moving.

"I'm sorry. I didn't mean it," I wailed.

Natalie awkwardly patted my shoulder.

"Don't tell Mom," she said. "She'll kill us."

"Okay," I gulped.

Handing me a sliver of a Hershey Bar she'd been saving, she said, "Come on, let's go home. We're going to be late."

We didn't bother to make sure we had no chocolate stains on our faces. My mother wasn't noticing trifles like that anymore.

My father decided we were going on a Sunday drive to Connecticut. "That'll make you glad you live in the city," he joked.

I squinted at Ava to catch some indication of whether we were going to have a good time or not. I could usually tell from whether she sat up straight or slouched. Her narrow back was fully erect, and a secret smile played on her face.

Good, it would be okay. Maybe her smile was because she'd just stolen some more costume jewelry from my mother's laminated box. Ava kept her stash on the top shelf of the closet in our room and only took it down to add new pieces or to admire them when no one was looking. I'd seen her one night when she thought I was sleeping. She'd first asked my sister in a whisper, "Natalie, are you asleep?" Then she tried me, "Tosca, are you awake?" but I didn't answer either because I thought she was going to ask me to do her a favor.

Through my half-opened eyes, I watched her tiptoe to her desk in the corner—actually, it was our desk, but she never let anyone else use it. I ended up doing my homework on the carpet, and my assignments were always full of tiny holes where my pencil poked through. She lifted the chair and placed it next to the closet door, lit a flashlight, and reached onto the shelf. I sat up so I could see better. She pulled something down. Sitting cross-legged on the floor, she shone the light into a box, and breathing noisily, held one piece of jewelry then another until the floor around her was covered in blue and red and purple stones. After examining them under the light, she carefully replaced each one back into the box. Then she retraced her movements, sinking finally into bed with a deep, satisfied sigh.

A thin wisp of blue smoke trailed from my father's cigarette into the backseat. I edged closer to the window and eyed the white lines in the road as they passed by in a blur. I already knew how scary the highway was. Anytime we went for a drive, everything looked out of control—cars careening all over the road, honking horns and shrieking brakes swelling the air. I pressed tightly against the window and concentrated on figuring out when we were going to be hit so I could warn the others. The white lines kept streaming steadily down the center of the road.

Then it struck me. The white lines were there to keep us safe. They provided an impenetrable border and stopped us from crossing over into danger on the other side of the road even if we wanted to. I observed how my father skidded and turned, stopped and started without a hitch and never strayed into the other lanes.

I relaxed back into the seat. We were safe. I didn't know yet that there weren't any white lines on my family's map.

After my father stopped off at a brick house to drop off a brown envelope, we drove right back home. Everyone was quiet, subdued. My parents barely spoke, and my father lit one cigarette after another, butt to butt.

"I have to fill up the tank," he muttered, turning into a gas station.

It was a relief to get out of the airless car. Natalie and I took off for the little store behind the pumps. My mother didn't notice and headed for the bathroom with Rock. The store was empty, and we sidled over to the candy aisle. I looked at Natalie. Natalie looked at me. Silently, she pointed her head to the shelf.

M&Ms? she indicated.

I shook my head. Too messy.

Sugar Daddy? Too obvious.

She passed me a slim yellow packet of Chiclets, and I slipped them in my pocket. We moved toward the door.

"Stop right there!" a voice shouted.

We froze. A large man in white overalls pushed in front of us and parked himself against the door.

I felt myself flush. Natalie's face creased with worry.

"What have you got in your pocket?" he asked, bending low so his face was in mine. A thin line of perspiration dripped down the side of his cheek.

Natalie's face puckered. "Please, mister," she said faintly. "We'll give it back. Just please don't tell my father."

The man slicked back his brown hair with wide fingers and squinted out the storefront. My father's deep, angry voice rumbled in the white heat across the space between store and pump.

"Figaro, go find your mother! And where the hell are Natalie and Tosca? Jesus, can't we go anywhere without losing everyone?"

Coins clinked in the man's pocket. A fan rattled in the background, pushing the stuffy air around the store.

"How old are you?" asked the man.

"Seven and a half," I answered.

"Ten," said Natalie.

He scratched his head; black half-moons lay under his nails. "I'll tell you what. I won't tell your father if you promise me one thing."

"Yes! Yes!"

"Promise me you'll never steal again."

"I promise!" Natalie said.

"Honest!" I cried.

"Remember what I said now," he called out after us.

"Remember what?" asked my mother, smoothing down her orange slacks before getting into the car.

"Nothing," said Natalie. She tightened her vise-like grip on my arm.

My father's head turned back. "Nothing comes from nothing," he said.

My mother laughed politely and patted his hand.

My heart still thudding, I went back to watching the white lines in the road.

Two strange men were hovering outside our building as we pulled to a stop. "Is that the FBI?" I whispered, breaking into a sweat. "What are they going to do to us?"

"Shh!" My sister yanked me so we fell into the middle of the family entourage. "It's okay. We gave it back, didn't we?" But she looked frightened.

The men followed us into the building and pulled my father aside as we waited for the elevator.

"Are you Aaron Ring?" one asked.

My mother's face blanched. "Go upstairs!" she hissed, pushing us into the elevator. She edged close to my father as the doors eased shut.

A cold hush filled the elevator as we gaped in bewilderment at one another. "I want Daddy!" Rock cried.

"Shut up!" Ava yelled. "Let me think!"

My parents' faces were white when they came back upstairs and disappeared into their bedroom.

"I told you it was a mistake to do it!" My mother's voice blasted through the door. "How could you declare bankruptcy just like that when—"

Her voice was interrupted by a loud thwack. My father must have hit the closet door again. "Goddammit!" he bellowed. "You've said enough!"

My flesh crawled. "Goddammit!" indicated that his rage had hit its peak.

Natalie slipped into the shower with me. "I think that was the FBI," she whispered, freckles standing out on her face like polka dots.

The soap shot out of my hands. "What did Daddy do?"

"I don't know."

My mother came out later with red eyes and made supper. We helped her wordlessly. My father stayed in the bedroom, shouting on the phone.

I put my head down like the others and played with my food until the meal was over. After supper, Ava washed, Natalie dried, and I put away the dishes. The boys emptied the garbage. I could never understand why that was all the boys had to do, like they were punished for being boys by having to do something that was dirty but, at the same time, rewarded by not having to do anything else.

We were all sent to bed, and for once, obeyed without complaining.

"Tosca, wake up! Come on, wake up!" Ava's nudging woke me from a deep slumber later that night.

"What time is it?" I mumbled.

"I don't know. Come on, you have to get dressed. We're leaving."

I shot up in bed, wide eyed. Natalie's bed was empty, her rumpled pink bedspread lying on the floor in a forgotten heap. Ava threw some clothes at me.

"Where are we going?" I asked. The Pepsi Cola sign twinkled across the black river.

"I don't know. Mommy and Daddy just said to get ready."

The apartment was ablaze with an eerie, unnatural light. In the center of the living room sat a mountain of boxes that my mother and father, bent over, sealed with brown packing tape. Natalie held the top of the boxes firmly shut, obediently moving her small fingers as the tape came closer. Marilyn lay screaming in a portable cot on the couch. Rock slouched on the floor, half-asleep.

My father's face was red. "Get over here," he yelled at Kirk who ran up and down the hallway, slamming doors. My brother froze, eyes dark and wide. Then he tossed his head and ran over.

"What about me?" Fig wailed, standing forlornly in the center of the room.

After my mother gave us each a suitcase to carry, we went downstairs to wait for a taxi.

"Where are we going?" I asked Natalie in the elevator.

She shrugged. Her eyes gleamed yellow in the dim light.

"I want to go back to bed!" Rock stamped his foot angrily. I tried to take his hand, but he pushed me away.

Two cabs screeched to a halt outside, and I piled into one of them with Natalie, Ava, Kirk, and Fig. My mother got into the other one, Marilyn crooked into her elbow and Rock dragged by the hand. The doorman stacked the suitcases on the backseat and in the trunk.

"Give me that briefcase. I'll take that," said my father. He stood alone on the deserted street, his eyes penetrating the cold blackness. Then, straightening his shoulders, he lit a cigarette and inhaled sharply. He turned back toward us and poked his head in the window. "LaGuardia Airport," he told the driver.

As we drove away, the doorman didn't wave but turned away and went inside, back to his newspaper at the front desk. I looked up. A light shone through the balcony way up on the penthouse floor.

"Hey, we forgot to turn the lights off," I said excitedly, tapping Ava on the arm.

My sister slumped into her seat. She stared morosely ahead. As we bounced along the throughway, my head fell back and I slid down the seat, lulled by the red lights streaming in front of us.

CHAPTER TWO

MEXICO

woke up shivering under a thin airline blanket. It was dark in the cabin, except for a single ray of light that shone over my father's head. His voice rose over the whirring of the engines.

"Will you stop worrying? It's all fixed."

The next time I woke, the plane had landed and my mother was soon pushing me down a metal staircase and into a low, pastel green building. The clacking of heels on cold concrete filled my ears. A crowd of people filed past a desk, opening and closing their passports. A thin blue haze of cigarette smoke hung paralyzed beneath the stark lights of the airport. My father had rushed off through passport control, to meet someone in the lounge about a house, he said, leaving us to deal with customs. His neatly polished shoes squeaked, and I wondered if my mother had remembered to pack his silk socks that had been drying in the bathroom.

My mother's hands looked brittle and shaky, and her face was streaked with old face powder.

"No, no money," she said over and over again at the customs table, rubbing her long palms together. "No jewelry, no perfume."

Her voice sounded measured, rehearsed, but the man in green uniform with a big black gun sticking out from his side didn't catch on and let us go.

In the taxi, I leaned against Natalie's shoulder. She gave me a twisted doughnutty-looking thing called a churro. I swallowed mine quickly before my mother could realize there was sugar in it.

"You like Mexico? You come for vacation?" asked the cab driver, smiling over his shoulder.

My father nodded coldly and lit a cigarette, discouraging further conversation.

I felt sorry for the driver so I piped up, "It was a surprise. We came from—"

My father's head turned sharply in my direction. "Be quiet," he frowned. "Go to sleep. You're tired."

The driver winked at me in the rearview mirror before focusing his eyes back on the road. It seemed that I was not the only one scared of my father.

A sudden lurch and the squeal of brakes jolted me awake. Surrounding us were rich green bushes splashed with red hibiscus flowers. A dirt driveway led to a house that my father called a hacienda, the word floating off his tongue like rain. Bright purple bougainvillea was everywhere, on the walls, along the bushes, branching up to the sky. My mother was going to like it, I could tell.

A woman with a gray braid and a blue-and-white-checked apron appeared from a small house on the other side of the driveway. Her head stooped as she helped us carry the luggage into the house.

The house was big, the color of a dusky sunset, and had a flat roof. Inside, a low-ceilinged living room sat at the center, off which led three large bedrooms, a kitchen, and bathroom. There weren't enough beds so Fig and I had to take turns sleeping on the living room couch, which cramped my legs.

"Where are we?" I asked sleepily.

"Cuernavaca, stupid," someone answered. But it didn't mean anything.

My father herded us into the living room. "If anyone asks you anything," he said, eyeing each of us in turn, "say you don't know." A muscle below his eye twitched like a fly had got caught in there.

"But Dad, you said it was wrong to lie," Ava said. She smelled like she'd been eating oranges, even though my mother had told us she didn't have any goddamn idea what we would be eating, not anything good and fresh anymore, that was for sure.

My father grinned tightly. "This is different," he said. "This is our own special game. Just say 'I'm glad you asked me that' and answer another question."

Kirk flinched at my father's wink.

Fig put his finger in his mouth and made a popping noise. "You're funny, Dad."

My mother's breath whistled like a train as she frowned at him, then at my father. "You're going to have to do better than that," she muttered as she walked off to the kitchen.

We had a whole family of servants now—María, her husband, Carlos, and Antonio, their fourteen-year-old son who was our gardener. Two black and white terriers, Chico and Chica, appeared as well. They yapped loudly and hurtled their small bodies in the air whenever anyone approached them, like miniscule guard dogs.

María helped my mother find a school for us. "The American School, it's very good, it's for people like you," she smiled, silver tooth glittering.

"Oh," said my mother, nodding seriously. "An American school. That's good." She found out the address, told María to make the necessary calls, and packed us off to school.

"Don't forget, it's spelled S-a-w-y-e-r," my mother said as I left for school.

My brow furrowed in confusion. "What did Dad say again?"

My mother tsked. "You never listen! They wouldn't let us in the country because they didn't like our last name so we had to change it." She glanced down at my sneakers. "Tie your laces." As if an afterthought, she added, "Don't tell anyone. They'll kick us out."

"Okay," I said, kneeling to tie my shoe. "Can I have a peanut butter and banana sandwich?" With the shutters closed against the morning sun, the tiled kitchen was dark and cool.

"There's no peanut butter," my mother said. "I made you

a hard-boiled egg instead." When she saw my expression, she snapped, "You should be lucky you have something to eat. People are starving in Europe."

I didn't know where Europe was, but I felt guilty and shut up.

"Don't forget—Sawyer," she said. She spelled it again. "If anyone asks you where you're from, say Alaska. If they ask what your father does, say you don't know." She handed me a plastic plaited bag. "Don't forget what I said, Tosca."

"Okay, Mom," I called over my shoulder as I ran down the driveway.

The other kids were already waiting, primed, in the school bus imported from the United States to take us to the American School. I imagined a tall brick building with a carved stone lion grinning over the entrance, just like my school in New York. The teachers would look like Mrs. Parker, with her sexy red dress clinging to large breasts.

A low building sat in the middle of a dirt field cast in an eerie whitish glow, its name the only thing reminiscent of where we had come from. Bathrooms were two outhouses, segregated by sex. My mother warned us not to touch the towels because, she admonished, they had hepatitis in them. No one spoke English or looked like us. The children wore blue uniforms—jacket and skirt for girls, jacket and pants for boys—and as they played together, they didn't seem to notice us.

My brothers and sisters disappeared into separate classrooms as I was led to mine. My classroom teacher indicated with a nod an empty desk by a window at the back when she saw I didn't understand a word of Spanish. I tried to smile at the other kids to show them I was normal but was greeted with hostile stares. Embarrassed, I turned away and looked dispiritedly out the window.

At the end of the day, the teacher sent me home with a note in Spanish. My mother asked María to translate, but she couldn't read so we had to wait until my father got home.

"You're going to have to buy the kids school uniforms," he read while loosening his tie. He took off his shoes, sighed, and spread his feet wide on the bright mosaic rug. "It's so hot. It took me half the day to find a car."

"Uniforms?" my mother asked, frowning. "Where do they expect us to find uniforms? Why can't they wear ordinary clothes like normal kids?"

My father shrugged. Later, we piled into his new white car and drove to the town square to a department store with green paint flaking on the outside. He dropped us off, saying he would come back in a while. A heavy-set saleswoman helped us compress our unwilling bodies into the stiff, confining material of the uniforms that made me itch. My mother, flustered, tried to order the large notes from her purse into payment.

With our packages neatly boxed and wrapped in smooth brown paper, we were herded back downstairs and onto the brilliantly sunny street. An old blind woman squatted against the corner of the building with her hand outstretched.

I stopped and stared at her faded brown eyes. "What's she saying?" I asked my mother.

"I don't know," she said, walking away.

"But Mom, she can't see!"

"Aw, she's only pretending," said Kirk, wiping his nose with a sleeve. "She puts stuff in her eyes to make them look like that."

"Why?"

"So people will feel sorry for her and give her money, dummy."

Why would anyone make themselves blind? I thought. I waved my fingers in front of her eyes to see if they would move. But her eyes remained motionless.

"She is *so* blind!" I cried.

"Are you coming or not?" my father yelled from the car.

I leaned my head back against the plastic seam of the car seat. Why would anyone choose to be blind? Were people really so mean, to trick others to give them money? My father's black head looked lustrous in front of me as he drove us away from town. What were we doing here anyway?

When I lay in bed at night, the thin, sharp ceraaaac-ceraaaaccing of crickets filled the cool night air. I didn't like sleeping on the couch with its frayed linen bedcover, but the sound of gently falling raindrops soothed me to sleep. Every night it rained and every day was sunny. In the morning when I dressed in my new uniform, the fragrance of dew-covered jasmine kept me feeling dreamy.

"The perfect climate," my mother sighed luxuriously, getting ready to lie in the sun as we took off for school.

The school uniform didn't make any difference, and I felt lonely and afraid at the back of the class. I kept my nose to the window, forlornly gazing out onto the treeless school yard.

"I don't have any!" Natalie cried one day after my father hit her for not doing homework. "The teacher doesn't even know my name!"

So my mother sent us to Spanish classes. She hired a tutor, Felipe, who lived on the other side of town. *Uno, dos, tres, cuatro, cinco, seis. . . ¿Cómo te llama? ¡Hola! ¿Qué tal? Es mi hermano, no, es mi 'ermano.*

Our teacher was young, with a wide swath of hair falling over his forehead and endless patience. Over and over again, he tried to coax our clumsy North American tongues to relax into Spanish. But he had to teach too many of us at the same time, and we didn't pick up much.

My mother didn't bother to sample our new language. She thought if she spoke English loudly and slowly enough everyone would understand, and were idiots if they didn't.

My father became a blur. I went to school and came home and took my turn sleeping on the small couch, and sometimes he was there, but often he wasn't. We didn't hold conferences, and I assumed my mother knew his comings and goings. But one day she ran frantically all over the big house and yard calling, "Aaron! Aaron!"

A rusty ladder leaned against the side of the house, and placing her hand on a rung, she rested for a moment. Then she continued her pacing in and out of the house, calling my father's name. We helped her, peeking behind the bushes, up the tree, at the back of the house, but my father was nowhere to be seen. Antonio grinned mysteriously but wouldn't say why.

Finally, Kirk climbed up the ladder and found him asleep, sunbathing naked on the roof. When Kirk came down giggling to tell my mother, I felt ashamed and embarrassed that my father had no clothes on. It made him seem vulnerable, not like my father at all.

One night, my father was in a good mood and took us to the opera in Mexico City. During the intermission, we crowded into the brightly illuminated bar, which had red walls and red velvet chairs. I went up to him as he laughed engagingly with a woman. She called him Aaron, and he chatted with her as though they were old friends. My mother stood beside them, smiling stiffly.

After the woman walked away, I pulled at his sleeve. My parents had told me they didn't know anyone in Mexico, that we shouldn't feel bad we didn't have any friends because they didn't either.

"Who's that, Dad?" I asked.

"Mrs. Whosiwhatsi." He smiled broadly down at me, dazzling under the radiant chandeliers of the bar.

I broke into a giggle. "Mrs. Whosiwhatsi," I repeated as I stood in the plush lobby of a beautiful theater that was as glamorous as my father. How lovely the ravishing color and heat of Mexico, how sweet the seduction of my father. I gazed up at him in fascination, the adoring fan to the grand opera of his life. But at the same time, a sliver of darkness broke through my father's illuminated image. Suddenly, I understood that we were in hiding, and that it was dangerous.

One Sunday, my father hired a driver to take us on a long, winding ride to look at some statues. We drove for hours up and down mountainsides, finally arriving at a vast expanse of field and brown brush that the driver said had been cleared away centuries before of its trees and wild vegetation. As we got out of the car I was blinded to everything but a huge staircase leading to the sky. Giant lions sat guarding it. We started climbing, one step at a time.

"It has 869 steps," said my father, reading from a guidebook.

A man and a woman holding hands passed us on the steps. "Honey, will you look at that?" whistled the man.

"Fabulous," she said. "Let's get a shot from the top."

Americans—I'd hardly heard anyone speaking English for a long time, not since we'd left New York.

"Hey, where are you from?" I called. "Are you from New York?"

My mother pulled me back. "Shh," she said, jabbing me in the ribs. "I told you not to talk to strangers."

"Why, that's all right," said the woman smiling as she reached into her bag. "Hey little girl, want some candy?"

I looked down, knowing what kind of trouble I'd be in if I reached out my hand.

"No, thank you," said my mother curtly.

The woman frowned for a moment, then caught up with her husband. Words drifted down to me as I followed them up the steps.

"Mother ... strange ... don't know why ..."

Her husband took her hand and drew her back into the safety of their world.

I arched my neck, viewing the way the steps gradually formed into a triangle. At the peak lay the rich blue sky and my father grew smaller and smaller as he climbed to the top. He became tiny in comparison to the stone and the sky and the lions, and I watched as he began to disappear into thin air. It was still and hot and quiet. He didn't look scary anymore, just a speck in the distance.

I turned around. The rest of my family receded in a series of tiny dots swallowed by the earth below. Suddenly, I felt that I might float away into nothingness. I tingled with fear—what would happen if my father disappeared altogether? In a panic, I began to climb.

"Dad! Wait for me!" My frustratingly short legs tumbled over the high stone blocks, but I kept climbing. Finally, breathless, I caught up with him.

"Why, Tosca," he smiled. "What a big girl you are, coming up all this way."

I didn't say anything but moved closer, panting anxiously.

We went to the market, came home, ate, slept, went to school and Spanish lessons, ate some more, slept again. Life went on. We had no plans, none that I knew of, and it could have gone on forever. But then, one day, we came home from the store and it was clear something was wrong as soon as we walked in the front door. An unfamiliar air hung over the living room and had the faint smell of something unrecognizable. I was sure I had made up the couch in the morning—my mother always checked—but the sheets and blankets were rumpled.

"Aaron," my mother said hesitatingly, but my father was already on the move. Throwing down the grocery bags, he dashed into the master bedroom.

"Stay here," my mother commanded, and followed closely behind. "Oh my god," she shrieked. "What have they done?"

I went to peer unseen through the open door. Clothes, papers, and dresser drawers were strewn all over the floor. The bed was in pieces, the mattress in shreds on the floor, pillows slashed, the white lace bedcover heaped in the corner, covered in feathers. Books had been thrown viciously against the wall, the threads of their thick hemp bindings blasted through.

"I can't believe it!" my mother moaned, crouching on her knees over her broken but still full jewelry box. My father ransacked through everything, looking for what might be missing.

"Goddammit," he yelled through gritted teeth, hair flapping over his flushed face. "If I find out who did this, I'll kill them."

I shrank deeper into the door frame.

"But how did they find us?" my mother wailed. "No one was supposed to know we were here."

My parents talked behind the closed door late into the night. First they said it was Carlos or maybe Antonio, but at the back of their minds they were worried about something more dangerous. After all, nothing had been stolen. Someone who was out to get my father was looking for something. I curled up in my bed-couch in the living room, worried about what was going to happen to us.

I woke when the room was still shrouded in black, to the sound of my father talking into the phone in the corner. Every so often he raised his voice, "*¡No, el primero!*" I kept my breath shallow so he wouldn't know I was awake. After he hung up the phone, he shook me. "Wake up. We're getting out of here. Put on your clothes. The taxi's going to be here in twenty minutes."

Chico and Chica set up a wail as we crept out into the lightly falling rain. Rock tried to run back to scoop them up, but

my mother grabbed his arm and shoved him into the awaiting cab. I could hear the dogs' shrill yapping as we left the
driveway, sped through Cuernavaca, out of Morelos, through
Mexico City, and onto a plane headed for another place I'd
never heard of.

I don't remember packing or saying good-bye to anyone, not
even Antonio or María. Some time later, we arrived in Nassau.

CHAPTER THREE

THE ISLAND

M om, are we staying here?" Natalie asked after we'd gone through customs and waited at the Hertz Rent-a-Car counter. Nassau turned out to be an island. I saw it from the airplane.

"What are you asking me for? Why don't you ask your father?" She flicked her nails impatiently, then pushed Rock away from her legs.

"Dad, did we move?" Natalie said.

"No." His eyelids drooped in fatigue.

"Are we in America?" asked Kirk.

"No. It belongs to England," my father answered distract-edly.

"How can one country own another one?" I asked.

He signed a piece of paper and took the keys from the assis-tant. "I'll tell you when you're older."

"You're so stupid," muttered Ava. "Don't you know any-thing?"

"Well, if you know so much, why don't you tell me?" I said hotly.

"Shut up, everyone." The hat on my mother's head tilted to the side, making her look like she was about to topple over as we followed her into the car lot.

The car sucked in stinging hot air that smelled sharp and sweet, like burnt grass. As my father drove I stared out the window. We passed by flat fields with tufts of yellow brush and swaying palm trees. A row of low shacks huddled along the roadside, their walls and roofs plastered with holes, like no one lived in them. Then we came upon a street busy with shops, traffic, and people.

"This looks like Main Street," said my father, scanning the map resting on the steering wheel. "We must be almost there."

I sat up at the sight of the ocean that appeared behind a crisscross metal fence and gazed at the water, feeling like I was very far away. The only time I had seen the ocean was when I was three and my parents had taken us to Virginia Beach. On the shore had been a float bobbing up and down. When no one was looking, I climbed on. The deep blue of the water became darker, its coating shimmering like glass as I drifted farther out to sea. It was quiet and calm. Without warning, a huge splash erupted out of the water and a man rose up, almost tipping me off the float.

"What the hell do you think you're doing?" he screamed. I gaped at him, skin prickling with fear. He tugged a corner of the float, gasping as he pumped his thick muscles back to shore. "You dumb—little jerk—getting every—one all—worried—like that."

Everyone but my mother. Some women on the beach had seen me disappearing into the horizon and had run for the lifeguard.

After staying in a hotel in the middle of town, we moved on to a street that continued up from Main Street, into a neighborhood dotted with white houses, front lawns, and open cesspools at the back. We were the only ones who weren't British. My parents tried to make us fit in. Our last name was now Smith.

"Yes, both my husband's and my parents were English," I overheard my mother telling the Tubbses, our neighbors who lived on the other side of the vines erected to keep out strangers. Brown, flaking leaves covered the path as one ivy after another choked in the unrelenting heat, but the Tubbses were stubborn and kept on importing them from England. Sometimes, safely hidden by the flora, I ran whooping back and forth under the arch to annoy them.

"Oh really?" Mrs. Tubbs asked, eyebrows raised, thin lips pursed as tightly as the bun on the back of her head. "And my, you're so dark! What part of England were they from?"

My mother's chin jutted out and she smiled brightly. "I really must go. I have so much to do. All those boxes to unpack."

I knew it wasn't true—all we had brought to Nassau were suitcases.

"Mom?" I tugged her skirt as we ducked under the vines. "Were you born in England?"

"Don't be silly," she snorted.

"Are your parents in England?"

A stinging slap landed on my cheek. "Shut up, for Christ's sake! What is it with you?" Twisting my ear, she marched me upstairs to my bedroom and slammed the door.

If I had known then what England was like, I wouldn't have bothered crying as much as I did that afternoon. Right now, though, England seemed different, an exciting, rich place that owned other countries and where there were people like the Tubbses who wanted to know as much about my parents as I did.

We started our new school—but first we had to buy new uniforms. They were brown this time. It was an English school, and we were the only foreigners. The school was divided into four discrete buildings called Houses, each with its own motto inscribed in Latin that no one could understand above the stone front entrance and marked by different emblematic colors—red, green, blue and yellow. The classes were divided into forms, not grades like in New York. There was Red Form 1, Green Form 1, Blue Form 1, Yellow Form 1, and so on up the grades. On the first day, my family was split up into different Houses. I was placed in Red Form 3 and warned to associate only with pupils in my House.

"This will prepare you for the outside world," said the headmaster, waving the cane that he used to rap errant students on the knuckles.

Outside in the dirt school yard, I wandered over to where my brother and older boys gambled with marbles. "Hey, let me play," I said, ducking low so the roaming prefects wouldn't catch me consorting with other colors.

"Okay," Kirk answered, covered in dust. "But you've got to put in marbles first."

"But I don't have any."

He thrust three small marbles at me. "Use these."

I got down on my knees as they did and shot at a row of marbles lined up against the side of the building. I missed every shot, so I went to play with Natalie and her friends, who were trying to jump off the shed roof without breaking a leg.

"Go on!" shouted a thirteen-year-old girl who had been kept behind in Natalie's class because no one knew she needed glasses. A girl with lanky brown hair paused halfway up to the roof.

"Crikey, you'll make me fall!" she giggled nervously.

Sweating in the heat, I squinted up at her figure silhouetted against the hazy blue sky. She seemed mountains above us. Then she whizzed down, flailing her arms like a big turkey, and landed on her feet with a soft thud.

"I want to go next," I cried, pushing past Natalie who was next in line.

Natalie shoved me aside, but her great descent was interrupted by the loud ringing of the bell that demanded our entry back to class.

The Callaghans lived across the street from us. There were three kids, Frances, Mary, and Theresa, and they went to a Catholic school instead of ours. When Mrs. Callaghan was angry, she washed their mouths out with soap and hot chili sauce. At first, it scared me that she didn't just hit them with a ping-pong paddle as my father did. But then I figured that's what Catholics did.

Theresa was my friend, Mary was Natalie's. Theresa and I played with her dolls, but I preferred Mary. She was muscular and strong and lassoed her hair into a tight ponytail that bounced from side to side as she wiggled up and down her room. She pored over women's magazines with my sister, learning how to be a Real Woman. Her room was shrouded in lipsticks and face powder scrounged from her mother. Her deepest regret—aside from the fact that her mother was fat—was that she had freckles, so she spent hours applying heavy layers of sticky pink Anti-Freckle Creme that clashed horribly with her orange hair.

Mary reported that a woman had to have three diamond shapes in her legs to be perfect: one at the middle of her thighs, one below her knees, and a third above her ankles. She began the competition for the Perfect Legs.

"You have to keep your feet straight," she commanded, her forehead covered in thick white grease to prevent wrinkles, even though she was only eleven.

"I don't want to play," whined Theresa, picking a scab off her elbow.

Mary laughed scornfully. "Of course not, you twit. You're too fat anyway!"

"I hope the Virgin Mary shits on you," Theresa muttered, storming off to her room.

Mary ignored her. "Look at my legs. See the diamonds?"

I stared at her long legs. There they were, three perfect diamonds between two wondrous legs. I sighed. How could I compete?

Placing my feet firmly parallel, I bent down and examined my legs. No diamonds. I tried again, this time pulling my feet apart a little. Still no diamonds.

"Show me again," I said, frustrated.

She smirked and repeated her movements.

"But you said to keep your feet together!" I said.

"I did, stupid!"

"You did not! I saw you!"

"I did so. Look!" And she did it again. But her feet stuck out, like a duck's.

"Mary, look! They aren't together." I was puzzled. Maybe she couldn't tell.

Mary laughed smugly. "Huh," she said. "Guess I won." She slung her hair back and rolled upstairs.

I stood there with a strange feeling in my stomach. Why did her feet look like they were poked out when she said they weren't? I walked home slowly, confused, believing and disbelieving her Perfect Legs at the same time. It felt just like my father hitting us if we lied but ordering us to lie if anyone asked questions.

At supper, Ava put down her fork and said, "Dad, are we going to move again?"

My father looked surprised. "What do you mean?" he said. "This is our home."

He had a new business partner, Bruno, a man who came to visit soon after we settled in. I could tell my mother didn't like him from the way her head inclined when she said his name.

"He has a whole houseful of cats," she said. "It's disgusting."

"What does he do?" asked Ava.

My mother turned away. "Oh, just business."

Bruno smelled like cabbage left too long in the refrigerator. He puffed on a cigar, blowing thick smoke into the hallway when my father answered the door. Thin and pale, his wife stood behind him, shrinking into the door frame like she didn't want to be there while Bruno and my father slapped each other on the back, laughing loudly.

"Bruno, meet my kids." My father pointed at us as he went down the line.

"What a cutie!" Two fat gray fingers pinched my cheek. I wiped off their imprint as Bruno scrutinized my face with a grin. "You look just like my pussycat Emelda. Want a little kitten? Maybe your Daddy will get you one."

My father smiled politely and went on to introduce Fig.

"With all these kids, who needs animals?" said my mother behind his back.

When Bruno went out of town, he asked my father to look

after his oldest cat, who needed extra care. We drove over to pick it up, and my father stuffed the squealing ball of gray fur into the trunk of our convertible. The luckless animal must have been plotting its revenge because as soon as we arrived home and my father opened up the trunk, it gave a mighty yeowl and shot out like it was on fire.

"Good riddance," said my father after poking halfheartedly in the bushes for a few moments. He must have concocted some story for Bruno on his return to explain the cat's disappearance.

"You think that man is going to change your life?" my mother hissed after dark the night of Bruno's visit. The hot, humid air made my pajamas stick to my legs.

"What are you talking about?" The gravel in his voice showed how angry he was. "It's business."

There was a pause, during which my heart beat so loudly I thought they might hear me crouching on the stairs. The lamplight threw my parents' reflections on the wall into shadowy relief, and I held my breath, waiting for my father to go on. After a long while, he cleared his throat and spoke quietly, softer, calmer.

"Listen Lucille, this is a sure bet. We'll be back where we were, can't you see?"

"I don't know." My mother crossed her arms in disbelief. "How do you know the same thing won't happen?"

A blue flame flickered next to my father's jaw as he lit a

cigarette. "Just leave it to me. Everything's fixed. It'll work out. Don't worry." He rose to his feet. "Come on, let's go to bed."

My mother shook her head. "I don't know, I don't know if I like you working with that man. He seems fishy to me."

My father laughed. "You can say that again!"

My mother's scowl grew deeper. "Very funny. I think a fish farm is a bunch of baloney if you ask me. And why does he need all that money?" She reached under the table lamp and snapped it off. Her shrill tones rose in the dark. "If this so-called scheme's got that much profit, what does he need you for? That's what got you into trouble in the first place. The wrong people. How do you know you can trust him any better than those other guys?"

I had never heard my mother talk to my father like that. Usually she reserved her irritation for us. I felt clammy— was my father going to hit her? But all I heard were their footsteps moving toward the bedroom and the door clicking shut.

I sat on the stairs for a long time, hearing the sighs of my sleeping brothers and sisters. A forgotten baby bottle gleamed at the foot of the stairs as a ray of moonlight appeared through the uncurtained window of the living room. I knew we had to be nice to Bruno because he was helping my father. But did my father know Bruno was lying? "Gambling," I thought Bruno had said to his wife while my father was out buying more beer and we helped my mother cook T-bone steaks. He had laughed sarcastically in the living room as I carried silverware to the table. "Of course he'll buy into it. Gambling is a thing of the future. Don't you know that?"

"Get away from that door," my father frowned when he'd come back with the beer. "Haven't I told you eavesdroppers have their ears cut off?"

n Nassau, the raw smell of the ocean was never far away. In my sleep, I dreamed that I went down to Main Street by myself and climbed over the fence to the sea. The beach lay vast and unspoiled with not a soul around to ripple the still air. I felt happy, calm. One wave after another washed gently over the smooth white sand as I stooped down to dab my fingertips in the water. I strolled farther, feeling a warm breeze tickle the hairs on my neck. Without warning, a huge tidal wave appeared out of nowhere. Gathering speed, it galloped toward the shore, a giant mouth swallowing up everything in its path. Panicked, I turned around to run away. Instead of there being Main Street, another monstrous giant of water was rushing at me from the other side. I shrieked for help, but no one came. No one was there. My screaming brought me back to my dark room, drenched and shaken, while my family continued to sleep soundly in their beds.

Now that my father was back in business, he was back in business—with a brand-new red paddle. We were no longer allowed to eat sugar. On the first day of school, Kirk got into trouble for drinking a Fanta.

"But Mommy, it's just like Orange Crush!" That was what we had drunk by the crate load in Mexico.

"So what?" my mother said angrily. "You just wait 'til Dad gets home."

Natalie and I stole into the snack shop at school and swiped penny candy, called sweets, during recess. Once, I stole a big grape bubble gumball. I hoarded it in my pocket all day, and when I got home, snuck it underneath my pillow so I could savor it after dark.

My father was in a good mood at dinner. "Pass the salt, sweetie."

I quickly grasped the shaker and slid it to him at the other end of the table. He hadn't called me that since I was three. He chuckled and forked another mouthful of chicken salad into his mouth.

"Things are looking up, kids," he said. "Your father's going to be bringing home the bacon like nobody's business."

"What about Bruno, Dad?" A deep furrow made its way across Ava's brow. "Do we have to see him again?"

Ice clinked noisily in my father's glass as he took another sip of his drink. "Of course," he said quizzically. "What's the matter? Don't you like him?"

Ava and Natalie exchanged looks. Then Natalie piped up, "He smells."

Fig burst out giggling. "He smells like cat doo-doo!" he said.

My father pretended to look angry. "Oh, he's not that bad. He just has a case of catitis."

"What's that, Dad?" I got ready to laugh.

"Oh, you know, when you have a cat you end up looking like them."

"You mean smell like them," my mother quipped. Still wearing a hat from when she had gone to the market, she looked tired as she spooned baby food down Marilyn's throat.

Rock held his sides together and roared, "Ha-ha!"

Ava cast her eyes skyward, sighing heavily. She never thought anything was funny anymore.

After dinner, I rushed off to bed. I was all ready to reach under the pillow for the bubble gum when the door opened and my father came in. His face was rosy and his eyes were bright. "You've been such a good girl, I've come to tuck you in."

I looked up at him, flushed with love and anxiety. Maybe he wouldn't see the gum if I angled myself carefully under the sheets. But he leaned over and lifted the pillow to plump it into shape. And there was the gum, fully exposed, big, round, and purple.

"Why you little . . ." he said.

I covered my head with my arm, waiting for the blow. He stood silently, glowering, while I felt the wash of his disappointment flood through me. I kept my head protected, but he didn't move, just stayed there staring at me. Then he quietly strode out.

After the door closed, I placed the gum in my mouth for comfort. But it didn't taste how I had imagined it would, and terrified about what my punishment would be, I sucked in vain as it turned into a sodden mass in my mouth.

The next morning, my mother glared at me as she handed me my lunch box for school. "Rats eat gum, you know. They creep into people's bedrooms at night and jump up onto the bed. Then they crawl under the sheets and bite them."

"What did she do, Mom?" asked Fig, puckering up his face. He'd been scared ever since a rat had run across the floor when he was on the toilet. The door had been locked so no one could help him—not until my father took a flying leap against the door and crashed inside. Then, with my brother in his arms, my father had charged into the hallway, screaming. I didn't know what Fig was more scared of—the rat or my father's scream.

"None of your business," retorted my mother. "Eat your food."

That was the last time my father tucked me in, and the last time I ate gum in bed.

n New York, we'd had piano lessons. In Mexico, we'd had Spanish lessons. In Nassau, we didn't have any lessons at all. Except one.

One day on our way to the fish market with Natalie and my mother—not a market at all but an old wooden wagon stuffed with slabs of salty-smelling fish—I peeked between the metallic lines of the fence dividing the street from the sea and saw a man sitting on a beach chair, gazing quietly at the calm blue sea. His hands rested on his hard, round stomach, his fingers wrapped loosely together. A white haze poured from the sky onto the water, sending sparks of light to the waves. It was warm and balmy. Usually, a soft breeze blew through the palm fronds that lined the street, but today the air was completely still.

"Can I go to the beach?" I asked.

"May I," snapped my mother. "No, that's only for the natives."

"What are natives?"

"People who live here," she frowned.

"But we live here!"

"That's not what I meant. Come on, get moving, we have a lot to do."

I looked at the man differently. His skin was reddish and black at the same time, like the roasted chestnuts we used to buy on the street in New York.

"Hey, look! That man got burnt by the sun!"

My mother wrinkled her nose in disgust, catching Natalie's eye. "Some people are born like that," she said.

Natalie looked down her nose and said, "Stupid. They were in New York, too. Don't you notice anything?" She glanced at my mother for approval.

My shorts and tee shirt were drenched from the heat. I held my hair off my neck as I read my book on the couch, *The Secret Seven on the Trail*, concentrating so hard I didn't hear my father's tread.

"Tosca, do you want to come to the store with me?"

I looked up eagerly. "You want me to come to the store?"

"Yes. Hurry up!"

Running out the side door, I shouted, "Mom, I'm going to the store with Dad." She was on the porch with Natalie, sewing. Marilyn slept in a basket between them.

My father was already sitting at the wheel in his red convertible with the roof down. I had never been in the car alone with him.

"Sure you don't want to stay here with us?" my mother called. "I'll teach you how to sew. I'm showing Natalie."

My eyes swung back and forth between my mother's hands and my father's car.

"Come on!" My father adjusted his mirror and revved the car.

I looked back at the porch. My mother leaned closer to Natalie and gave her a long piece of thread. Natalie smiled and straightened her back.

"I'm staying with Mom," I called over my shoulder and dashed up the steps.

"Okay," my father said, and drove out the driveway.

Then I remembered I hated sewing. It was boring.

"Wait, Dad!" I raced to the car before he could make his turn. "I want to come with you!" Maybe he'd let me sit next to him in my mother's seat.

But my mother said she wanted me, too.

Dizzy, I cried, "What should I do?"

My mother's face was blank. "What are you asking me for?" she said coolly.

My father's voice floated behind me as he revved up the car again. "Make up your mind!"

"Okay, I'm coming with you!" I ran to the car and jumped in.

It didn't matter that my father played music loudly out the car radio. It didn't matter that we passed a store that had a picture of the man who was singing—Nat King Cole. It didn't even matter that my father forgot the sugar rule and bought me a chocolate ice cream. I could tell I didn't really matter one way or another.

Deb Butcher lived in the neighborhood with her father and older brother, Derek. Their mother had disappeared somewhere. Deb never said where, but one day when I went over to play, I heard her father scream, "You're just like your mum, a bloody whore!" Deb whipped out of the house without seeing me and ran into the bushes, tears streaming down her face.

Their house wasn't painted and had rotting wood inside and out. I felt sorry for them and tried to be friends, even though their house was dark and scary and down a steep hill from our house.

"Come on," leered Derek one rainy day. "Let's have a pajama party!" Thin brown hairs covered his upper lip, and he smelled damp and rubbery.

"Okay," I said, curious about what a pajama party was.

"You can wear my pajamas," said Deb, reaching under the bed. She had a strange look in her eye. "Leave your clothes on."

After I put on the pajamas over my clothes, she said, "Get on the bed. Derek will tell us what to do next."

I giggled as I crawled under the covers with her. The rain pounded on the roof, reminding me how fun it was to play Thunder and Lightning under the piano with Kirk and Fig in New York.

Derek said, quietly at first but gradually louder, "I'm the bogey man and I can do whatever I want."

"No!" screamed Deb, clutching my hand.

"Yes, I am, and I'm coming to get you!" With a terrifying roar, Derek trampolined onto the bed and crashed onto me full force.

"Let me up!" I choked, trying to push him off me.

"Don't go," Deb pleaded in a frantic whisper. "Stay with me. You'll be okay."

"No!" I struggled to climb out of the sheets.

"Where are you going?" boomed Derek, forcing a pillow over my face. I kicked my arms and legs wildly as blackness beat down and suffocated me.

"Help! Stop it!" I tried to scream and bit into thick pillow instead. My body iced over and I lay completely still for a few moments. Then a blinding force ripped through my chest and I catapulted into the air, knocking Derek off balance. I jumped off the bed and ran out of the house and all the way home through the torrential rain. Deb's pathetic little voice echoed in my head as I raced up the hill. "Tosca, don't leave me. Don't go."

Natalie stood in the living room with her arms outstretched, singing along with the radio. "I love you for sen-ti-men-en-tal rea-he-son-hons—"

"Derek threw a pillow over my head and wouldn't let go!" I cried.

Natalie looked over with glassy eyes. "Why are you all wet?" She drew closer. "What are you doing with those pajamas on?"

"Natalie, Derek tried to strangle me!"

My sister's hands flapped in the air. "What do you want to play with them for anyway? They're dirty."

She came with me to throw the pajamas down the cesspool, and I never went back down the hill. When Deb came up looking for someone to play with, her legs covered in scratches, I pretended I didn't see her. I ran behind the house, overcome with guilt. I felt like crying because she looked so lonely. I knew it wasn't her fault, but I was too scared of her brother.

The Secret Seven were a gang who lived in England and went around solving mysteries, appearing in a series of books by Enid Blyton. They were always successful, they always said

"Blimey" just like the kids in Nassau, and each book ended with everyone happy—the parents, the children, and the people they rescued.

It fit—seven of us in the family, seven to solve a mystery. The only trouble was that only Kirk and Fig would join my Secret Seven club. Roger Tubbs from next door and Mary and Theresa were roped in. Then we pulled three-year-old Rock away from his toy truck and forced him to play, just so we would add up to seven.

Huddled together in the low concrete shed at the back of our house, we began our first meeting by making up rules. The shed was near enough the cesspool to force us to close the door against the smell, adding deliciously to our secrecy. Just as we got to our fourth rule, No One Else Allowed In, a huge wasp squeezed in through the door and buzzed ferociously in our faces as it zipped from one corner of the room to the other. My father, woken from his afternoon slumber by the noise of seven screams, burst into the shed with a rolled-up newspaper lit like a firecracker. He waved it around, yelling at us to keep out of the way. We ran out under his arm, one by one, as he propped himself at the entrance. The thick black smoke drove out the wasp, but we were too terrified to go back inside—ever again. The Secret Seven Go AWOL.

What do you want to sleep over at Theresa's for?" said my mother, frowning as she loaded socks into a bowl.

"She asked me to," I said. "Please, Mom, let me go."

"I don't know," she said. "It's better for you to be home."

"But it's only across the street," I begged.

"Stop whining!"

"Please, Mom, please let me go."

She tsked tiredly. "Oh, all right. You can go after supper when you're ready for bed."

At eight o'clock, I stumbled in my pajamas across the pitch-black road to Theresa's house.

"Why," her mother said, looking surprised under the hallway light, "Theresa's already in bed. I thought you were coming for dinner before your sleepover."

"My mother told me to wait until I was ready for bed."

"Hmm," said Mrs. Callaghan, wrinkling her forehead. "Usually her friends come over before dinner." She slapped me lightly on the butt. "Anyway, away with you. She'll be glad you're here."

"I thought you weren't coming," said Theresa, looking up from her dolls. She put them one by one on the floor beside her and got into bed.

"Where should I sleep?" I asked.

She lifted her bedcover for me to get in beside her. Then she yawned and turned out the flashlight. "Good night."

"Don't go to sleep yet," I said. "Tell me a story."

"I'll tell you one in the morning," she mumbled.

I lay in the dark to the sound of her breathing, straining to reassure myself that the dark shadows looming in the air weren't monsters. When they grew closer, I jumped out of bed and ran down the stairs and out the door back to my house, tripping on my pajama bottoms.

My mother laughed as she saw me plunge through the front door. "See?" she said. "I told you you're better off at home."

Kirk and I had just finished a game of marbles and were pretending to ignore the bell calling us back to class when my father arrived in the school courtyard. He looked at Kirk, not seeming to notice me frozen to the spot.

"Get your things. We're moving."

"I don't want to move again," Kirk whimpered, twisting his shirtsleeve with his fingers.

My father lit a cigarette and blew it to the side. "Come on, everyone's waiting."

"Daddy, I don't want to go. Don't make me go. I don't want to go. I just made new friends. Please, Daddy, don't make me go."

My father took his hand away from his eyes and pulled him along. "We have to," he said gruffly, reaching for a large handkerchief in his back pocket. "Here," he said. "Blow your nose."

It was quiet in the cab where everyone waited for us. Natalie hadn't been at school because she was sick. After the engine started up, she put her mouth close to me and wheezed into my ear, "Mom said Bruno stole all Dad's money."

"What?" I mouthed silently, gesturing with my head at Kirk so he'd know to lean closer and hear it, too. He kicked me.

"Ouch," I yelped automatically.

"What's going on back there?" cried my mother swiveling around, her mascara smudged under one eye. "Be quiet, all of you."

Natalie waited until my mother had turned around again, and leaned her face into mine, her breath hot and moist on my mouth. "Then the taxi came and Mom said we had to get out of here."

Through the back window, I peered numbly at the school yard emptied of children called to class by the bell. Thin lines lay in the yellow-brown dust where we had been playing in the marble court. Farther back, the four Houses stood silent and tall against the sky, with part of the shed jutting out. Now I'd never get my chance to jump off the roof with everybody hearing me screaming.

CHAPTER FOUR

SINUS TROUBLE

We moved into a small brick house on a street somewhere in Jacksonville, Florida, in the middle of the night. The dimly lit rooms were small and square, already full of furniture. My mother allotted the rooms quickly and sent us to bed.

"But Mom, I don't want to sleep in there," said Kirk, his voice hoarse from crying.

"Just go," she said, pushing him.

The next morning when I awoke, it was cold and frost lay on the harsh ground. The surrounding houses sat in rows, some red brick, some wooden painted over in whites and grays. Outside lay identical squares of grass. Everything looked flat, like the life had been ironed out by the colorless sky. My mother was mad.

"It's supposed to be warm in Florida!" she complained. "My sinuses are killing me already."

My father ignored her as he lit a fire in the hearth. Marilyn was propped in the middle of the floor, eating a page of a magazine. Rock and Fig raced toy cars around the couch, shouting and whistling. Ava and Natalie were still sleeping, and I went off to wake them up before my mother could tell me to start doing chores by myself.

Later, I found my father alone in the breakfast room. His hair and face were rumpled, but I didn't care that he hadn't had his coffee yet. I stood by the door.

"Dad, why did we have to come to this place?"

He arched his eyebrows. "What are you doing here?" he asked. "You should be helping your mother get the kids ready."

"Ready for what?" I knew we weren't going to school. It was Saturday.

My father looked blank for a moment, then scratched his head. "What do you want from me?" he said tiredly.

The look on his face made me feel like crying. I wanted to help him stop feeling sad. I waited, wondering what to do. Then I remembered how Kirk had looked in the field at school in Nassau when my father had taken us away. I stamped my foot.

"Why are we here?" I screamed.

My father's eyes narrowed, and he turned red from the neck up. "How dare you talk to me like that." He raised a fist. "You'd better get out of here before I—"

I fled.

joined school in the middle of a semester and the middle of a class. My teacher was called Miss Bernstein, and she smiled cheerfully as I was ushered into the room by the principal. A smattering of freckles lay over her large, aquiline nose. Brown hair framed her sallow-skinned face, and around her neck lay a beige and gold scarf. Her breasts stood out like sharp cones in a smooth expanse of starched, white shirt. She reached up to rub her nose, wrinkled it, then did it again. I stared at her, fascinated.

"Class, this is Tosca," she said. "Tosca Walters, is that right?"

I couldn't remember what my last name was, so I nodded.

"Tosca just moved here." Miss Bernstein nodded at me encouragingly. "Go on, tell the class where you moved from."

I remembered my orders not to say anything and bowed my head.

Miss Bernstein rubbed her nose again. "Well, that's okay. We'll get to know you soon enough." She turned to the class. "Tosca's mother said her family came from here and she always wanted to return," she said brightly. "Now isn't that nice?"

I scowled and toyed with my new pen against the edge of the wooden desk.

Miss Bernstein clapped her hands sharply. "Okay kids, back to work. It's time for our spelling quiz."

I looked up, excited about a spelling bee. I hadn't been able to take part in a spelling contest since we left New York. I walked over to line up by the wall. Someone tittered.

"You don't have to stand up," said the teacher. "Just raise your hand when you can spell the word correctly."

Blushing, I slid back into my seat. The classroom was warm and light with its white walls and large windows. Drawings and embroidery hung everywhere. A coat rack, nailed tightly to an area by the door, was marked with names carefully inscribed in childish handwriting. Underneath, coats and jackets were roughly hooked. I didn't have a sweater and pulled my shirt-sleeves down, cold at the change in climate.

"Spell 'said,'" Miss Bernstein read out from her primer.

I frantically waved my hand in the air, scared she wouldn't notice me.

"Tosca?" she smiled invitingly.

"S-a-y-e-d," I spelled confidently, proud to be such a good speller.

"I'm afraid not, Tosca. That's not the right answer." She looked around the room. "Anyone else want to try?"

I shrank back, humiliated. S-a-i-d. I knew how to spell it. Now all the kids were going to think I was stupid.

A cross the wide, barren street from my all-white school in this place as segregated as Nassau sat a corner drugstore. A cash register rested above shelves displaying colorful candy bars. Beside it lay a spiky rubber oval, on which the storekeeper placed change in nickels and dimes. A long, shiny counter and faded plastic stools faced the glass door. The only black person in the place was Freddy, a teenager who worked behind the soda counter. The storekeeper's face was always red from yelling at him, "Hey Freddy. Get moving! There's customers waiting."

I didn't know why he kept yelling—Freddy never stayed in

one place for more than a second. I felt like telling the store-keeper to shut up. He was the one who was always slouching around, doing nothing. But something on Freddy's face told me not to. Besides, as long as the storekeeper focused on Freddy, I could swipe as much candy as I wanted.

Kids from my school went in groups to sit at the counter, drink Cokes, and eat ice cream sundaes while they waited for their mothers to pick them up. My mother said I wasn't allowed to have any and to wait for her outside. But I went in anyway, on my own because Natalie had started junior high school.

Outside the drugstore stood a large red scale shaped like a lollipop. The aluminum circle around its face read in num-bers the horror of the women who, after glancing around to make sure no one was looking, shoved a penny in and bal-anced themselves precariously on its platform. A small mirror was placed just above the face, and when I was bored, I would stare at myself, savoring the sweetness of my newly snatched candy bounty. My nose was growing faster than the rest of me, and I rubbed it like Miss Bernstein as I waited for my mother to come. One day, I had only just managed to wolf down the last bite of a Mars Bar and slip outside to the street when my mother appeared, impatiently clacking her heels on the hard cement.

"Hi, Mom," I said, nonchalantly. I swallowed hard to make the last of the lumpy caramel filling disappear down my throat.

My mother turned her head. "What have you been up to?" she asked, lips pursed.

"Nothing," I answered, wondering how she always seemed to know when I did something wrong.

"Are you lying to me?" she asked.

"No, Mom, honest," I pleaded, my arm shielding my head.

But she only narrowed her eyes. Abruptly, she turned toward the bus stop while I tripped over my feet, trying to keep up with her angry stride. The clacking of her heels collided with the hiss and growl of the bus. We got on, not speaking.

On the way home, my mother indicated a church near the bus stop. I followed her in and sat obediently next to her. She had started dropping in on churches on the way home ever since we moved there.

"My father was a minister, you know," she said. She thought for a moment, then added, "Presbyterian."

She didn't care what kind of church we visited, as long as there was music. While we sat in a pew and listened to a choir practicing or organ music grinding heavily in the close atmosphere, my mother's features smoothed out and she closed her eyes, tapping her foot in rhythm. I sat quietly, scared she'd get mad if I interrupted her.

Back home, she threw off her camel-colored woolen coat. "Look in the mirror," she snapped.

I glanced in the glass hanging over the telephone in the dark entrance hall.

"What do you call that?" she snorted, gesturing at my mouth.

In the corners lay the remnants of my Mars Bar. There was

a big to-do that night when my father got home, and I was sent to bed without any supper.

Thereafter I stuck to M&Ms. I thought they wouldn't do to my face what they weren't supposed to do to your hands.

n the middle of reading us a story, Miss Bernstein was interrupted by a loud rapping at the door. The air was crisp outside, but the classroom was toasty with its warm brown linoleum floor. The sun pouring in through the aluminum and glass windows cast brilliant streams of light through the venetian blinds.

Miss Bernstein looked up, entranced, the tip of her nose red from rubbing. She moved quietly to the door, the soft soles of her shoes conforming to the No Stilettos signs all over the school. The principal was furious at the scratches on the linoleum floors that even heavy layers of wax couldn't prevent. He had called us all for a special assembly to inform us coldly that stilettos were forbidden. I didn't know why he called in the children—none of us wore high heels.

Miss Bernstein opened the door. "Yes?"

I felt a nudge. "Hey, got any gum?" my neighbor hissed, flipping back her straight blonde hair.

"No," I whispered back, and tried to concentrate so I could hear what was going on outside the classroom, stomach tingling. Was it my father? Were we moving again?

Miss Bernstein finally came back. Her face looked ashen.

"Class," she started, but then her voice broke. "The president has been shot!" Her legs buckled and she unsteadily tried to regain control of herself. "Put your heads down," she choked, "and we'll say a prayer so that our president lives."

I breathed a sigh of relief and twisted around to watch what people's faces looked like when they talked to something that didn't exist.

"Our father who art in heaven," the children repeated after my teacher, "hallowed be thy name . . ."

I rubbed the tip of my nose, feeling grown up that I was the only one not crying.

The door burst open. "President Kennedy is dead!" shouted a boy.

"Oh my god!" Miss Bernstein cried. With long black streaks of tears pouring down her face, she dismissed the class, ordering us to hurry home.

That night at supper, my mother served spaghetti, orange with tomato paste. After propping the transistor radio on the sideboard, my father said, "That whole family was a bunch of crooks."

"But Dad," said Ava, wiping her mouth with a paper napkin, "at school they said he was doing good things for everyone. Civil rights and everything."

My father sneered. "Civil rights, my . . . All he ever cared about was who he was going to prosecute next."

"What does prosecute mean?" I asked.

No one answered. From the radio, the sound of a man incanting in a strange tongue sent Rock into giggles.

"Who's that on the radio?" I said, raising my voice.

"It's a priest, dummy," said Kirk, kicking me under the table. "That's what Catholics do when someone dies."

"It sounds funny," said Fig, screwing up his face. He held his nose. "Yonniny donniny doo."

Everyone laughed, including my parents.

My mother said, "He was a crook, investigating people like Dad for nothing. If it wasn't for him, Dad would still be working at the stock market and we'd still be—"

"You're right, he was a real con man," my father interrupted, giving my mother a warning look.

"Like Bruno," nodded Ava, mouth full of spaghetti.

My father's chair scraped back, leaving an angry sound in the air. "What do you know about Bruno?"

Ava's face puckered, but she didn't answer.

A few days earlier, my mother had been talking to her in the dining room, not knowing I lay on the floor under the table. I had been thinking about Theresa Callaghan. I missed her and her stories but didn't know her address to write. When I had asked my mother, she acted like she'd never heard of her.

"That Bruno was a gangster," my mother said to Ava above my head. "You know what he did?" Her voice rose in a thin wail. "He told Dad he had this business and Dad—you know him," she interrupted herself angrily, "he never was a good judge of people—he believed him and gave him all his money. That crook swindled him out of all of his money!"

After a pause, Ava asked, "Does Dad have any left?"

My mother had grunted in irritation. "Stop asking questions."

Now, my father's lips were tight. We all looked at him, tense, alert. But he merely cleared his throat and went back to twirling spaghetti around his fork. His hands still looked waxy, but since we had left New York, he didn't wear clear nail polish anymore. In the light, his fingers appeared red, brutish, strong.

He poured another drink and my mother turned up the radio. During the rest of dinner, we kept laughing, convinced we were better than all the nincompoops in the country who my father and mother thought were too stupid to know "what's really going on."

discovered I was growing breasts on the same day that Fig held a birthday party. That was because a friend of his shot a dart at my nipple from a dart gun. When I took my shirt off to look, I found hard, swollen bumps on both sides.

"Mommy, can I have a bra?" I asked excitedly.

"Don't be ridiculous," she said. "You're only eight."

"But Mom, look." I held up my shirt for her to see. Natalie had a bra and I wanted one, too.

"Oh," tsked my mother, turning away. "That's nothing."

I slumped out of the kitchen, feeling angry and stupid. I went to sit dreamily by the window, gazing at the strange haircuts and smooth white faces on the black-and-white cover of the Beatles LP my father had brought home.

"Ugh," my mother said as she walked through the living room carrying a tub of fresh laundry. "What a bunch of noise."

Against the background of "Love Me Do," her radio in the kitchen blasted opera. She always played it loudly, like she wanted to drown herself—or us—in it.

After a few seconds she came back, muttering, "Idiots."

My back tingled every time she crossed the living room floor. It didn't matter though—my father liked the Beatles and so could I.

My sisters and I listened to the record over and over again, conjuring up the Fab Four throwing their arms around us and kissing us on the lips. Ava chose Ringo as her true love, John was Natalie's, and Paul had fat cheeks, so George was left over for me. Besides, he had a big nose like me and looked sad. I felt sorry for him, and clutching the album cover, I swore to love him forever.

I didn't want to go out of the house once we had the Beatles. I was happier lying on the floor, rubbing my nose like Miss Bernstein and feeling the songs take me far away. In any case, I was scared to go out in case I got lost.

I didn't make school friends. It was too hard when I wasn't allowed to eat ice cream with them after school. My mother got sick of me and the Beatles so, throwing her coat on, she walked me around the neighborhood. At four-thirty in the afternoon, almost every house had a kid playing outside.

"Go on," said my mother, pushing me toward a blonde girl perched on a wall with a Barbie doll in her hand who looked about six years old. "You're friendly. Tell her you want to be her friend."

"Aw, Mom, she's too young," I protested. "I don't know what to say."

"Just tell her your name," she admonished, brandishing a Kleenex from her purse. "Damn sinuses. Doesn't it ever get warm here?"

I knew better than to argue. "Hi," I said, choking with embarrassment. "My name is Tosca. What's yours?"

The girl stared at me. I scuffed my sneakers.

"Do you want to play?" I asked hesitantly.

"No," she said flatly.

"Go to hell," I mumbled, turning on my heel.

"What did you say?" My mother slapped me.

"She doesn't want to play," I whimpered with my hand on my head.

"Oh, come on!"

Outside the next house, three boys in thick blue overalls and red windbreakers played catch with a baseball and mitts.

"Uh—" I started, but my mother pulled me to the next house where a girl my age was pushing a toddler on a makeshift swing in their yard.

The girl shyly averted her gaze and let me push her sister on the swing.

When I turned back to my mother, pleased with myself, she was gone.

We moved right after that. We had lived in Jacksonville for only three months. I overheard my mother tell Fig that we were going south, where there wasn't any sinus trouble.

CHAPTER FIVE

THE HURRICANE

A naked lightbulb hung in the motel room over two narrow single beds and a light brown wardrobe. The room smelled musty, like cold, damp earth. The orange and green bedspread matched the sign flashing Howard Johnson through the pitch-black night. My father searched his suitcase while drinking from a paper cup.

"Can I have some?" I asked.

"No, you're too young," he said. From the blank look on his face, I could tell he was listening with only half an ear. Muttering under his breath, he placed the cup high on the wardrobe and strode out of the room.

I pulled over a chair and reached for the cup. I choked as the fiery liquid hit the back of my throat. It tasted bitter and foul, just like the way I felt about being there. After carefully replacing it exactly how he had positioned it, I sat back down on the lumpy bedspread with a sour feeling in my stomach and waited for him to return.

He told us we were in Florida, but it didn't feel like Florida.

Here where we were staying until he found us somewhere to live, it was dark and dingy but also warm, humid, not frosty like Jacksonville.

The man behind the front desk had said, "Welcome to Miami Beach, kids!" after our night flight, when we had shuffled into a low concrete building squatting beside a highway whizzing with cars. His glasses flashed in the stark overhead lighting as my father grunted and asked him for three rooms.

"Where's Miami Beach?" I asked Natalie.

She rubbed her swollen eyes and yawned. "Mom said it's south." She picked up a suitcase and followed Ava and the boys back outside to our rooms. My mother blew her nose and told the clerk to have iced water delivered. Outside, an L-shaped courtyard pulsated with soft little insects. Crickets chirped nearby, and it felt like we were back in Nassau. Only the way the desk clerk sounded told me this was somewhere different.

We stayed in the motel for two or three weeks. It was hard to tell how long as time drifted by meaninglessly, the days unseparated by shopping or going to school or helping my mother in the kitchen. After we found somewhere to live, my parents sometimes took us back to the motel for dinner or ice cream. I consoled myself by stealing wads of saltwater taffy from the counter while the others hunched over in adjoining booths, not speaking, faces mournful beneath the garish lighting.

———

While we waited at the motel for a home, my mother took us on a long bus ride. The hot, sticky air made my hair cling to my neck. We got off near a carpet warehouse and obeyed my mother's orders to follow her inside.

A thousand rolls of rugs hung in straight rows from the ceiling, smelling like wet sweaters. My mother sneezed a couple of times, then fetched a handkerchief from her purse and kept it to her nose as she inspected the merchandise.

"It's so humid," she complained.

A man came forward from the back of the warehouse to pull the carpets back and forth on their massive overhangs.

"No, purple," my mother said, tapping her foot. Her fingers twitched nervously on the clasp of her purse.

The man frowned. "Purple. Oh yes, come this way."

"Hmm" was all she said after a lengthy pause. Then she shook her head. "Can't afford it anyway."

We followed her back out, along a street lined with desolate cement warehouses. At the end of the street, to my surprise, lay the sea.

The ocean was cast in an eerie gray light, reflecting a sky full of thick, unmoving clouds. White foam spit at the sand as one wave after another rolled in. My mother scanned the beach and then allowed Ava and Natalie to go off on a walk down the promenade. She made me and the others stay with her. The boys fought about where to build a castle while Marilyn struggled on the sand, feeding chunks of it into her mouth. I squatted next to my mother, watching her remove her black strapless shoes and dangle them one against the other as she cast a vacant look at the water. Broken Coke bottles and torn candy wrappers littered the beach.

"Mom, can I have an ice cream?" I asked casually.

"No," she grumbled, and halfheartedly pulled Marilyn on her lap. I sighed and burrowed my feet deep into the sand. My sisters had disappeared and I was too bored to play with the boys.

"Where's Dad?"

"So many questions." My mother pulled a magazine from her purse and leafed wearily through the pages. She never said much anymore. She was always tired and I was scared to bother her; well, not scared exactly because she hadn't slapped me for a while, but the nothingness it brought made me feel even worse.

I lay back and stared at the sky. Tiny black dots fell like feathers in front of my eyes. I tried to trace their descent, but no matter how much I concentrated, they scattered like gnats in the humid air. Farther down the beach strode a woman in a yellow dress, cut into a sharp V down her chest. She held hands with a little girl who was jumping up and down.

"Lemme go in dah wadah, Mama!" the girl called excitedly.

The woman beamed and raced her to the waves. Ava and Natalie, back from their walk, passed them, snickering behind their hands.

"Lucille!" my father called down from the boardwalk.

My mother gathered her belongings and told us to hurry, and we climbed the wooden steps toward my father leaning hard against the railings. Unlotioned and uncombed, the row of waves in his hair had disappeared.

We piled into a cab and drove to a short street with only one house on it. On the other side was a golf course. We turned into the driveway lined with trees. At the end sat a dirt-streaked garage with two large windows overhead. To the right rose a rambling, U-shaped five-bedroom house edged by a slanted porch littered with dead leaves. A mossy pond, also covered in leaves, sat in the middle of the U, halfway between the house and the garage. It looked like no one had lived there for a long time.

"Look, Lucille." My father smiled. "Seven trees. One for each kid."

"But Dad, there's another tree over here," I said, pointing.

The tree he'd left out stood upright at the front corner of the house, layered with thick, leafy branches. It made the house seem rickety by comparison.

Kirk elbowed me. "That's an oak, stupid. He was only talking about palm trees."

My mother clapped her hands in excitement. This was much bigger than the house in Jacksonville.

"I used my credit teeth," my father said, grinning broadly at her unspoken question. He pointed to his front teeth. "When I show them these, they give me credit."

My mother threw her head back and laughed in delight.

———

was moved into the small attic room on the second floor. It had twin beds, but the room was all mine. When it rained, I woke up with water dripping on my stomach. My mother told me to move the bed and handed me a bucket to put on the floor until the leak was fixed. It never was, and on wet nights, I slept fitfully to the irregular drumming of water hitting metal.

Natalie and Ava were given the bedrooms over the garage and the boys the large room that bordered the driveway. My parents slept at the back and Marilyn in a little anteroom next to the living room. Our name was Turner, and we were the only people in the neighborhood who weren't Jewish. Or so my parents said.

Mom, I'm nine years old today," I said a few weeks after we moved into the house.

She looked up from cleaning the stove. "Really?" she said. "Happy birthday."

I strode into the living room where my father sat at the table, adding up numbers on a large piece of paper.

"Dad, it's my birthday," I said.

"Why," he said, stroking my head. "What a big girl you are. Can you ask Mom what time she wants to go to the market?"

"They forgot mine, too," said Natalie in the bathroom where I found her brushing her teeth. "Next time, tell them the day before. Then maybe you'll get a present."

———

My father drove us in his new convertible to a hotel at the center of town so we could learn how to swim. Mickey was the resident water ballet dancer at the hotel and had long black hair and a figure Mary Callaghan in Nassau would have died for.

"Just like Marilyn Monroe," whispered Natalie, staring at her. My mother wasn't so easily impressed and pursed her lips disapprovingly.

After my father introduced us, Mickey reached down and chucked me on the chin. "Hello there, Tosca," she said with a smile. "My goodness, what a grown-up name for such a little girl." Her breasts looked soft and squishy against the loose opening of her terry-cloth robe.

I giggled behind my hand, suddenly shy.

"Aaron, it's time for lunch," my mother said coldly, lifting Marilyn off the ground.

"Nice to meet you all." Mickey winked at me. "Make sure you watch closely now."

My father led us down a stairway to a bar shaped like a square doughnut. In the middle was a swimming pool, surrounded by glass. Wavy beams of bright sunshine filtered to the bottom of the pool, casting the bar in a ghostly turquoise light.

My mother pointed to two tables and made a waiter push them together. While my father ordered drinks for them and hamburgers for us, I pressed my nose against the window to get a closer look at the legs and arms thrashing just below the water's surface. An announcement came over the speakers.

"And now we have the most beautiful, the most graceful, the most acrobatic water dancer in the civilized world. Let's all welcome her with a big hand—Mickey Moore! The girl who stole my heart away and will steal yours, too!"

"I need another drink," said my mother, tapping her fingers. I was going to tell my father that my mother was talking to him, but when I saw the way he was staring at the pool, I changed my mind.

Through the window, Mickey bolted through the water. Her black hair flowed back and forth like seaweed, and lines of sunlight dappled her legs. She came right up to the glass, smiled and flowed away again.

"Remarkable," muttered my father, lips barely touching.

My mother glared at him, kicking her foot against the table leg. Every time she kicked, my tomato fell off my plate.

After the show, Mickey came downstairs and introduced us to her boyfriend. "Hey, you all, meet Ricky," she said. "He's going to teach you little ones how to swim."

"Ha! Mickey and Ricky," snorted my mother. "Aaron, I need a drink."

My father snapped his fingers at the waiter. "What'll you have, Mickey?"

Ricky and my mother exchanged looks, but no one said anything. Ricky was blond and rugged, and his thighs were covered in little curly hairs. When he was upstairs teaching us how to swim, Mickey sometimes came over to watch. They always laughed a lot, Mickey touching him all over. One day, my father invited them to the beach and I gaped as they showered off their hard, brown bodies. Throwing her head back laughing, Mickey reached a hand into her bikini bottoms and scrubbed. Ricky peeked inside, howling like a dog.

"Oh for god's sake," went my mother so loudly that the whole beach could hear.

Swimming for me was like all my other athletic pursuits. I tried hard. Kirk, on the other hand, excelled and joined the school swimming team. There was no point in trying to keep up, so after Ricky taught me the basics, I concentrated on developing my water dancing skills so I could be like Mickey.

Natalie became my ballet partner, and we swam the width of the pool underwater, pointing our toes and flapping our arms blissfully. When we got tired, we sat cross-legged on the floor of the pool and talked to each other in underwater language, bubbles bursting from our lips in rapturous laughter.

Every Saturday at two o'clock, the pool was cleared for Mickey's show. I was the only one who went downstairs to the bar every time. One afternoon, with my nose flattened against the glass, I viewed the surface of the water in anticipation. Whoosh—and in front of my eyes, she appeared as in a dream. Only this time, the top of her bikini whooshed down to the bottom without her.

"Hey, get a load of that!" someone shouted.

A crowd of men circulated to the window, grunting and snorting like pigs. Mickey's arms were up against her breasts, trying to shield them from view.

"Get lost," I muttered under my breath. I wanted to kill them. I tried to cover the glass with my hands so they couldn't see, but I was too short. Without her usual smile, Mickey disappeared to the surface. I was glad my father wasn't there.

My mother didn't walk me around as she had in Jacksonville, forcing me to make friends with the kids in the neighborhood. In any case, except for the Rosenbergs, there didn't seem to be any. The Rosenbergs lived around the corner from us. The day after we moved in, Mrs. Rosenberg knocked on our door and asked my mother over for coffee.

"Why don't you come, too?" she said, ruffling my hair. "You can play with my daughter, Becky."

My mother smiled and took off her apron. "We'd love to come, wouldn't we, Tosca?"

"Hi," said Becky, surrounded by toys in the middle of the living room. "Want to play make-believe?"

Becky looked like me with her brown hair and freckles, but she was only five. I taught her to look sophisticated by holding two fingers under her nose and rubbing like Miss Bernstein in Jacksonville. Then I went back to our street so I could play on the golf course by myself.

Mrs. Rosenberg thought I was cute until I peed on the wall outside her house as I sat waiting for her to take Becky and me to the beach. I was scared to ask if I could use the bathroom in case she changed her mind about bringing me, and even though I kept my legs tightly crossed, I couldn't stanch the flow of pee gushing down my legs. Becky was playing with her doll and didn't notice. I thought no one else would either, not until Mrs. Rosenberg stepped up to her car on the curb and told us to get in. I coughed to hide the sound of my squelching sneakers.

Peeking over her sunglasses, Mrs. Rosenberg asked, "Why are your shorts wet?"

I thrust out my chin. "They're not wet," I said.

She looked at me, then told me to wait. A few seconds later, she came back out of the house with a towel and placed it on the backseat. "You can get in now," she said.

On the way to the beach, my shorts dried and nothing was said. I never told my mother what happened. But it didn't matter anyway. She had already told me not to go over there.

"They're weird," she said.

I guessed she meant Jewish. That must have been why she had frowned when Mrs. Rosenberg laughed and said what nice Jewish kids we were.

D id anyone see my watch? I can't find it anywhere," said my mother, flicking a large fly with the sash of her new red gingham apron that Ava had bought her for Mother's Day. My mother had laughed scornfully when she had unwrapped her present, saying how unromantic household gifts were. But she wore it every time she cooked.

Ava had just scavenged the watch from my mother's bureau. I saw her place it in her new hiding place in her room above the garage. She wrapped the watch in the corner of her sheet, then stuffed it underneath the mattress. My mother complained that Evelyn, who came in to clean a few hours a week, had stolen it, but my mother was always losing things so no one paid much heed. Besides, Ava was clever enough to keep her things for only a short time so my mother wouldn't realize what was going on.

The skies had been dark and cloudy for days. According to the radio, from which my mother continued to blast opera, Hurricane Cleo threatened to hit us within a week. Our landlord, Mr. Carmichael, came over and hammered storm shutters on our windows, grumbling fiercely all the while. I sat in Natalie's room overlooking the driveway and watched the palms thrashing wildly, spraying their green spikes all over the place. Only the old oak refused to bend, standing fully erect outside my brothers' window at the front of the house.

Later, it started to rain, slowly at first, then thick and hard. We ate supper in silence, listening to hurricane warnings on the radio. The shutters flapped loudly against the windows as water dripped from a crack in the ceiling.

"Oh for god's sake," said my mother.

No one moved so, tsking loudly, she went to fetch a bucket.

My father lifted a forkful of roast beef and shouted over the roar.

"It's only a rainstorm. They're just sensationalizing it to get people glued to the radio so they'll listen to commercials and then run out and buy stuff." He snorted. "And then people get into car accidents because they're not thinking straight. What a bunch of phooey."

"My teacher said most accidents are caused by alcohol," said Kirk.

My father swung his fork. "That's ridiculous."

The sound of raindrops grew faster as they fell through the roof into the bucket. Plonk-plonk, like coins dropping one by one.

"It's true, Dad. My teacher said when people drink, they don't think and that's what causes accidents." Kirk's face was open, eager.

Fig laughed. "Drink, don't think. You're a poet and you don't know it."

The fork quavered in my father's hand.

"Hey, Dad, my class is having a competition," I said loudly. "We have to think of a slogan for the Department of Traffic for pedestrian safety. I'll get five dollars if I win."

My father cleared his throat as he put down his fork. My mother turned up the radio.

"We're expecting one-hundred-mile-an-hour winds," said the newscaster. "Stay inside. Parents, watch your children. Know where they are."

My father took a sip from his glass and chuckled. "We've brought you this far. We don't want to lose you now."

"Next time don't bother," muttered Natalie.

"What did you say?" My father turned red.

Plonk-plonk. Plonk-plonk. The room grew cold and I shivered, rubbing goose bumps on my arms.

"Nothing, Dad."

Ava stifled a grin and kept eating.

"I have to make up something for the competition by next week," I said, raising my voice. "It's to stop children getting run over. They're going to put up a big sign for everyone to read."

"How about 'Don't get in the way of cars,'" said Kirk.

"That's boring," said Natalie. "What about 'Keep your head and you won't lose everything else?'"

My mother laughed hollowly and stared at my father. "That's pretty good, 'lose everything else.'"

"I know," said Ava. "Look out or you'll get that rundown feeling."

"Very good," nodded my father. "I think you should enter that one."

A loud bang came from the window. Everybody jumped.

"Aaron, go fix the shutter," urged my mother.

"No, Dad, don't go. The man on the radio said it was dangerous." With a twisted face, Rock looked at my father pleadingly.

My father chuckled and took another sip from his glass. "Guess I'd better stay then."

After supper, my mother turned on the television. It was our first one. My parents didn't believe in television—not until Ava persuaded them she needed it for school. That was after she said her teacher was upset because my mother didn't turn up for the PTA meetings. I sat on the floor and watched the news announcer point at a map and show with circles where the hurricane was expected to hit.

Bang! Bang! I huddled closer to Natalie on the floor and kept watching the announcer with his pointer. "If we're lucky," he was saying, "we won't have too much damage. Just enough to keep us busy for a while."

"Bang!" shouted Fig. We all jumped again.

"Shut up!" I said. "It's not funny! We could be killed. What if the house blows away?"

"Oh, don't be so serious," said my mother, turning up the television.

Plonk-plonk-plonk-plonk. Plonk-plonk-plonk-plonk.

The announcer said, "Half the county has already had a power failure. If you're still watching, do not be alarmed if your TV set goes off. We'll come back on the air just as soon as we can."

The flinging of water against the shutters sounded like crashing waves. Suddenly the picture on the television screen shrank to a tiny white dot at the center. And then that, too, faded, leaving us in utter blackness. Marilyn started crying.

There was a whishing sound as my father lit his lighter. "Where are the candles?"

"We don't have any." Ava's voice echoed in the darkness.

"Okay, everyone." My mother clapped her hands. "Time for bed. Ava, Natalie, Tosca, you sleep in here. It's too wet in your rooms."

I was surprised. I didn't know their roof leaked, too.

My father kept flicking his lighter, cursing under his breath as he led my mother and the other kids to their beds. I spread myself across two chairs—Ava took the couch and Natalie another two chairs next to me—to the banging and howling and whooshing of the hurricane. A sudden crack made the house shake.

"I'm scared," I whispered.

"It's okay. Go to sleep," Natalie mumbled. The chair creaked as she moved into a different position.

I kept shifting to try to get comfortable, and just when I thought the howling would never stop, everything went scary quiet.

"What happened?" Natalie whispered, jolting upright.

I untangled myself from the chairs and tiptoed outside with her. My father rested against the side of the porch with the boys, pointing at the eerie green sky. The air smelled like rotten eggs. All around us lay branches and leaves and thick clods of earth that had been tossed brutally in the air, and yet here we all were, safe and solid and sound. The storm seemed to be over and our house was still standing. I sat on the wooden slats of the stairs, chin in hand, listening to my father explain how hurricanes worked, coming in a big rush and then nothing.

"We're in the eye of the storm," he explained.

As I listened to him, I guessed it was true what he had said, that we were safe in Miami Beach. I'd heard him telling my mother that the other night, and it looked like he was okay because he was never home during the day. Maybe everything would be fine. Maybe we wouldn't have to move again. Perhaps this time we could stay where we were.

A clap startled me as the skies burst open again. As we raced inside for cover, it sounded louder and crazier than before, like it had only stopped to catch its breath and was now trying to smash us to pieces.

In the morning, I straggled out with the others to see the damage. The air still smelled like rotten eggs, but the sky was no longer green. The courtyard was covered in branches and palm fronds that had been ripped out of their sockets, and the pond had been emptied out. Green moss and dead tadpoles were strewn everywhere. The hurricane had squashed a part of our house so it looked lopsided, and the roof tiles, already loose, had been angrily pried away in the storm and lay at our feet. The storm shutters hadn't been strong enough to withstand the one-hundred-mile-an-hour winds, and all the windows on the front side of the house were broken. At the corner of the house, the big old oak had been torn from its roots and was now splayed across the driveway. If it had fallen the other way, it would have landed on Kirk's bed.

My mother folded her arms and laughed mirthlessly. "There's no place like home."

———

The weather had returned to normal, and Natalie and I climbed out of my bedroom window to count wooden beams through the holes in the roof. Once we were perched at the edge overlooking the courtyard, she reached into her pocket for a small blue book.

"Hey, Tos, look at this."

I leaned over her shoulder and read in my mother's spidery handwriting, "I don't know how much more of this I can take. How did he ever get us in this mess in the first place? I thought it was a good idea, leaving New York until the trouble was over, but this is ridiculous. How does he expect me to manage with a houseful of kids and him never home? And all the money's gone. I must be an idiot to put up with it. I swear, if it wasn't for the kids, I'd kill myself. If I don't kill that Mickey first. How dare she flirt with him, right in front of me?" My mother's handwriting grew sloppier, with smudges around the letters. "I've had enough. Enough! It's more than anyone can take. If only it wasn't for the kids."

Pots clanked below as my mother cooked supper. Natalie looked at me, shading her eyes against the sun. "What do you think?"

I read it again, fascinated. It didn't sound like my mother. She never talked like that.

"I don't know. Let's put it back before she catches us."

Natalie stuffed the book in her shorts at the sound of a car pulling up in the driveway.

"Hello, Mr. Carmichael." I waved to our landlord emerging from the car. He looked up, then turned red, like he was about to explode. With a growl, he charged into the house. I stared at Natalie, not sure what I'd done wrong.

Mr. Carmichael appeared with my mother next to him. He had her by the arm and was gesticulating wildly at us. "That's why your roof leaks!"

My mother tilted back her head. Her hair wasn't combed and fanned her face like a bird's nest. "So, you never heard of the hurricane?" she said. "If you'd done a good job in the first place, this never would have happened."

"Just pay the rent, Mrs. Turner! And get those kids off the roof!"

My mother shook her fist in the air. "I'll pay you when you do some fixing around here! The roof needs repairing, the wallpaper is falling off the walls, and the water is orange when it comes out of the pipes. You fix and I'll pay!"

But he was already tearing down the driveway in his car. "You're already three months overdue!" he shouted out the window, then vanished around the corner.

My mother stood for a few minutes not looking at us, then bowed her head and disappeared back into the house.

———

A few weeks later, Kirk found me on the swings in the neighborhood playground by myself, daydreaming with a book in one hand. The sky was glowing pink and gold in the dusk as he tapped me on the shoulder.

"Hey, you have to come home!"

"Why?" I frowned.

"You won the traffic safety competition! A newspaperman came to take your picture. You won five dollars!"

As I raced home the sprinklers on every front lawn were on full blast. I landed by the photographer at our front entrance, soaking wet. Throwing my hands to my face, I said, "I can't believe it!"

"That was a great slogan you entered," said the newspaper reporter. "'Look out or you'll get that rundown feeling.'" He chuckled.

My mother pulled me aside, nodding politely at the photographer, hand to my head as if she wanted to smooth my hair.

"Don't forget," she hissed in my ear. "Your last name is Turner. If you say anything else, Dad's going to be in a lot of trouble and we'll have to move again."

My scalp prickled. I turned to the photographer.

"I just can't believe it," I said again.

He said, "No, do what you did when you first came home. Put your hands up to your face and look surprised."

I did what he said, automatically, as he clicked his camera. My mother stood beside me and said I looked adorable, with a frozen smile on her face.

———

A family that plays together stays together, read the sign. My mother had bought it in Woolworths, embroidered it when we were at school, and placed it above the stove. Then she started a tradition of making us have supper together every night, my father included. We had to wait for him to come home before we could eat.

"But, Luce, I can't always be back on time," he complained behind the kitchen door.

"Just see what you can do," replied my mother. "I need help with the kids. They're driving me crazy."

Fig and his friends had climbed onto the roof and bet on who could pee the farthest. My mother had forced Natalie and me to spend the rest of the day squirting bleach on everything. We had run off halfway through and disappeared across the street to the golf course. When my mother came to look for us, she had stumbled over Kirk smoking cigarettes behind a bush. Ava was in her room sulking so my mother was left all on her own to clean up the mess. An evening get-together was her attempt to make things more manageable.

Marilyn was the only one who was excused from supper duty. At two years old, she was sleeping in her anteroom by the time the evening meal rolled around. Everyone else had his or her set place at the long formica table. Mine was in the middle of one side, between Kirk and Fig, who still had a row of thin welts where my mother had slapped him with her bony fingers.

Ava, Rock, and Natalie were lined up on the other side. My father sat at the head and my mother at the foot.

"Maybe Ava can go in and help you after school," said my mother, mixing the salad at the middle of the table.

My father glowered at her. "What are you talking about?"

"You know, in your office."

"Hmm . . . yes . . . my office."

"My teacher wants to know what you do, Daddy," said Kirk.

My father's face darkened. "Tell her to mind her own business."

"But Daddy, everyone has to write a story about their family."

"What's your teacher's name?"

My mother interjected. "Just tell her he's an insurance salesman."

"Ha, yes, an insurance salesman. That's good." My father wiped his mouth with a napkin. "As if I'd ever stoop so low."

"So why don't you have Ava help you in the office? That way she can learn something instead of pouting in her room all day." Her lip curled derisively.

"Very funny," said my father.

I looked swiftly at Ava. Her face looked sulky and defiant at the same time. She threw down her napkin with tears in her eyes.

"You never let me do anything! All you ever do is make us move! I hate my school! I don't know anybody! I'm sick of it!"

My father's eyes narrowed threateningly. "Sit down!"

My sister glared at him in hatred.

A thick blue cord rose like a river on his neck. "Do you think I like this any better than you do? I'm doing this for your own good!" He waved his knife in the air. "Listen, you ungrateful wretches! I could have left you alone with your mother. She would have had to go on welfare. You want that? Is that what you want?"

No one dared to say anything. My mother glanced accusingly at us.

Clearing his throat, my father continued in a menacing whisper, "Do you think it's right for a father to leave his wife and children?"

The grating of my mother's chair sent a shiver down my neck. "You should be thankful. How dare you talk to Dad like that. Don't you know how hard he's working to support you?" As one, my parents rose to their feet and stalked out of the room.

"Bastards," Ava muttered through clenched teeth. "Just you wait."

Natalie and I cleared the dishes, trying not to make a sound.

I didn't know my father did this for us. I didn't know what he did. But if he said it was for us, I had to be grateful. Whatever welfare was, it sounded scary. I didn't know whether I preferred my father with us or not. We didn't really have a choice.

A few days later, when I got home from school, a strange

man sat in the worn velvet armchair by the front window of the living room. He was stuffed into a dark blue suit, muscles bulging through the fabric. I ran into the hallway.

"Mom, I'm home!"

My mother came out of the kitchen, speckles of grease on her apron, hushing me with a frown.

"Be quiet! Dad's sleeping!"

"Who's that man?" I whispered, following her into the kitchen.

She stirred sauce into the pot on the stove. "I'll tell you when you're older. Help me with the salad."

Afterward, I escaped to Natalie's room over the garage. "Who's that man in the living room?" I asked.

"What man?" Natalie asked.

Ava heard me from her adjoining bedroom and strode in. "Did you see Dad?" she asked, straddling a chair.

"No. Mom said he was sleeping."

"Ha," Ava snorted. "Just wait 'til you see his face!"

"What does he look like?" said Natalie, gaping at her.

"His face is all black and blue. Someone beat him up."

"Who?" I asked, stunned.

"I don't know." She bit her nail. "I heard him telling Mom it's about money, but she wouldn't say anything. That guy is going to follow him everywhere. He's a bodyguard."

"I thought only presidents had bodyguards," I said. President Kennedy had had lots of them and he was dead.

Ava sighed irritably. "Well, stupid, now Dad has one, too."

My father was gone from the house when we awoke, and so was the bodyguard. My mother said my father was away on business. When he came back a few days later, he looked normal. Except for the occasional presence of the bodyguard who sat in the living room when my father was home, I forgot that he'd been beaten up. The man, who never introduced himself, faded into the background. Soon I hardly noticed him at all.

I walked in on my mother while she was swallowing a handful of little yellow pills. "What are those, Mom?" I asked.

Her eyes shifted. "Don't worry your little head about it."

At the hotel, I found her sharing a bottle with Mickey. "Here, kiddo, take some of these," she said to Mickey as she poured the pills into her hand. "What does he matter anyway?"

"Who, Mom?" I asked.

"Mind your own business," she slurred. "Go back in the swimming pool."

All through supper, my father drummed his fingers against the table.

"What's the matter?" my mother said as she poured him a drink after we'd gone. She thought we were all in bed. "You don't want your little girlfriend high as a kite?" The tone of her voice was a mixture of laughter and weeping.

"You don't know what you're talking about," my father answered icily. "She's a business associate."

"If I ever catch you . . ." My mother's voice drifted off.

I climbed up to Natalie's room. "Is Mickey a bad person?" I asked.

"No."

"Why doesn't Mom like her?"

"Who knows?" she said, sounding bored. "Mom doesn't like anyone."

Coconut trees swayed in the wind as we rode down a wide street to the supermarket. People with shopping bags floated alongside, easing in and out of stores like driftwood. In our white convertible, my father's hair shimmered in the bright sunlight, a line of grease at his collar. Blue strands of cigarette smoke drifted to the backseat where I sat as far away from Fig as I could. I was still mad at him because his friends chased me all over the yard calling me fatty. Instead of coming to my protection, he had hooked up the hose and sprayed me with cold water. Now we had to help my parents go shopping. Already my mother was nervous and irritated.

The night before, my parents had argued again. "You pansy!" my mother had screamed as I'd helped Natalie carry Marilyn's things to her room. The shattering of glass resounded through their bedroom door. My mother stormed out and ran upstairs to Ava for sympathy. They were still talking when Natalie, whose room was next door, went to bed.

"Mom thinks Dad's having an affair with Mickey," Natalie whispered after breakfast. "She said she's going to kill him if it's true."

My eyes widened. "What's going to happen to Mickey?"

Natalie shrugged.

Now, from the backseat, I could see my mother picking nervously at her nails. A thin hum came out of her mouth, matching the whine of the brakes as my father came to a stop and started up again. His knuckles blanched on the steering wheel, but he didn't say anything. This might be the best moment to ask, now that they weren't paying much attention.

"Can I have a bra?"

My mother turned to my father. "Do you think a nine-year-old should be wearing a bra?"

The car swerved sharply to the left. "No, I don't," he answered shortly. Just then a coconut landed on his head.

"Oh my god!" my mother screamed.

I fell off the seat as my father slammed on the brakes. But he quickly continued driving as if nothing had happened. My mother's voice softened as she stroked the back of his neck.

"Are you all right?" she asked worriedly.

The driver beside us shouted, "Don't worry, man, it's always happening to people on this street! Next time, keep the hood up!"

"I'm okay," my father mumbled, his hands fixed on the wheel and his eyes straight ahead. "I'm fine."

My mother giggled. "Wow, that was something. A coconut! We should've kept it and made piña coladas."

My father distractedly patted her knee and kept driving.

Fig stayed in one corner and I in the other, not looking at each other. "Idiot, think you're so smart," he said to me under his breath.

W ave your arms," my sister mimed in time to the music blaring on the gramophone upstairs in her room. "So come on, come on, do the Locomotion with me—"

"Like that, Ava?" I shouted, swinging my hips like hers.

"No, dummy, like this!"

"I know how to do it!" shrieked Kirk, flinging his arms out.

"Ouch!" Natalie bent over, clutching her side.

"Sorry!"

Fig appeared at the door. "Mommy's lying on the floor."

Ava stared at him. "Where is she?"

"In her room." He laughed. "She looks funny."

We followed him to my parents' bedroom and found my mother half-splayed off the bed, eyes closed and head lolling on the side. A patch of the brown bedspread was soaking wet, right near her legs. On the floor was a bottle of pills, and she clutched an empty liquor bottle in her hand.

We looked at her, not knowing what to do. A line of dribble lay at the side of her mouth. I wanted to touch her, to push her to see if she would wake up. But I couldn't move. Fig broke into nervous giggles. Natalie turned to him. Then she started giggling, too, and soon the rest of us were laughing uncontrollably.

Evelyn, the woman my mother had hired to clean the house every week, appeared with a quizzical look on her face.

"What's going on in here?" Her eyes caught my mother. "Oh my lord! I've got to get an ambulance."

She made us go back upstairs. After a while, a siren wailed outside our house and my mother was taken away.

When my father came home later, he gathered us in the kitchen. "Mom is taking a rest for a few days. We're all going to have to help out until she's back. Ava, I'm leaving you in charge."

"Okay, Dad," said Ava compliantly. "Do you want a drink? I can bring it to you in the living room."

My father looked at her askance. "No, that won't be necessary. Why don't you just get supper ready? Tosca, Natalie, help her with it."

"Can we visit her, Dad?" asked Natalie through pinched lips. I knew she was thinking about my mother's diary, just as I was.

"No, she needs to rest. Don't worry. She'll be home soon."

"Can Mickey come look after us?" I asked.

My father laughed shortly. "Certainly not."

When my mother returned home, she looked pale but acted as if nothing had happened. But we stopped swimming at the hotel and I never saw Mickey—or Evelyn—again.

———

M y mother and I arrived at seven-thirty for Mothers and Daughters Night at my school, even though the event didn't start until eight. My mother looked tired but in a relaxed, dreamy kind of way.

The large auditorium was only half-full, and we sat down in the third row from the front. I looked around, waving at my schoolmates, feeling part of something big. A girl from my class sat behind us, giggling with her mother. My stomach churned with excitement.

At eight o'clock sharp, the lights flickered and then came on again bright and strong. On stage, the principal tapped the microphone. Beside her stood a woman in butterfly glasses who held a naked white doll and a vanity case.

"Quiet, girls," said the principal. She smoothed her hands over her hips and coughed. "Welcome to our Mothers and Daughters Night! We have invited all of you here to learn about feminine hygiene. You girls are getting older—maybe faster than we'd like, eh, mothers?" She chuckled, and a few titters joined her from the audience.

"It's time you learned about feminine hygiene," she continued. "Miss Taylor is here to demonstrate what that means." She nodded at the woman next to her. "Please welcome Miss Taylor."

To loud applause, Miss Taylor stepped forward and told us we were becoming women and had to learn how to behave so that everyone knew we were nice young ladies.

"Young ladies speak softly and are polite at all times," she instructed. "Smile when addressed, and always wear the appropriate attire when you leave the house."

Miss Taylor held up a doll. "Now girls," she said conspiratorially, "imagine this is you. I am going to show you the correct way to wipe yourself after you go to the bathroom."

She reached into her vanity case and removed a huge wad of toilet paper. I sat forward, fascinated. I didn't dare look at my mother—she hated talking about anything to do with the bathroom.

Miss Taylor opened the doll's legs and slowly wiped its pelvis from front to back. "Front to back, girls!" she called loudly. "You don't want to be encouraging any of those nasty infections, especially after you start getting your period. See? Front to back."

I giggled, imagining everyone in the hall with her panties down. My mother nudged me sharply with an elbow.

"Any questions so far?" Miss Taylor swung her head from side to side, scanning the room for a few moments. "Okay, then, we'll continue."

A girl chirped indistinguishably from where I was sitting, but it sent the girls around her into a fit of giggles.

"Now, girls, this is a very serious matter," said the principal in a stern voice. "It's not ladylike to joke."

"Boy, if it isn't ladylike, who needs it?" my mother said out of the corner of her mouth. She looked at me and we both laughed, but only so we two could see. I leaned closer, light-headed.

"Any questions?" Miss Taylor repeated.

I thought hard. Maybe Miss Taylor knew whether ladies had to have three diamonds in their legs like Mary Callaghan in Nassau. I waved my hand frantically so I'd be called on, not realizing I was the only one with her hand up.

Miss Taylor's glasses flashed as she pointed to me. "I do declare, there's someone just bursting in her seat. Stand up so I can see you clearly, young lady."

Feeling all attention on me, I immediately forgot about the Perfect Legs. "Is it rude to rub your nose?"

Everyone laughed, including my mother. I fixed my eyes straight ahead, feeling like a fool.

"Rubbing your nose how?" Miss Taylor asked, bending down to view me more closely.

Reluctantly, I placed two fingers under my nose and pushed them side to side, just like Miss Bernstein, my teacher with the big nose in Jacksonville.

"No." Miss Taylor smiled. "That's fine. You keep rubbing your nose just like that!"

People were still chortling as I sat down. My mother leaned over and said, "You're cute."

I squirmed. I didn't feel very cute.

On the way home, I asked my mother what a period was. Flapping her hand vaguely, she told me to ask Ava.

When we got home, I ran up to my sister's room where she was poring over the John Lennon scrapbook normally hidden under her bed so no one could steal it.

"What's a period?" I asked.

Ava jumped, shoving the book under her pillow. "Didn't I tell you to knock first?"

I put my head down sheepishly. "Sorry." I waited a few seconds. "What's a period?"

The scar on Ava's lip turned a shade darker. "What are you asking me for? Ask Mom."

"She told me to ask you."

"How am I supposed to know?" She flounced off the bed. "Get out of my room. I'm busy."

M om, Marilyn's fallen in the pond!" Rock yelled from the yard.

My mother raced out of the house. She knelt by the tadpole pond and plunged her arms into the mossy water. Waving them about hysterically, she kept calling, "Marilyn, Marilyn!"

Marilyn appeared from around the corner, sucking on a handful of grass. Rock watched without expression. Then he laughed, "Only kidding."

My mother spun around and slapped him on the head. Then she stormed back into the kitchen, without taking Marilyn with her.

That night, I dreamed my mother was ironing in the Rosenbergs' house because our house had fallen down. Rock raced a toy car right near a slit in the floor. Suddenly, it widened and Rock disappeared inside. The hole closed up again, just as abruptly. My mother didn't notice. I stood by her side, pleading with her to dig him out. But she didn't hear me and kept on with the steady to-ing and fro-ing of her ironing.

I jerked awake. It took me some minutes to realize that I was only dreaming and that Rock was all right. But I wasn't sure that my mother would notice if the floor really could open up and my brother disappear inside.

Usually by seven o'clock, the boys were running up and down the hallway or my father was throwing a fit in the kitchen or my mother was yelling at Natalie and Ava to hurry up and get the younger ones ready for school. But this morning, a deathly hush hung in the air. My father had a headache. We crept around on tiptoes, putting on our shoes and socks and tying rubber straps around our books, waiting for him to drive us to school.

"Natalie, come here," my mother called around the kitchen door. "Kirk needs help."

My brother's hands were covered in large welts, rope burns from the day before in gym class. He moaned all night and woke up crying that his hands were on fire.

My mother told us to wait in the car while Natalie finished getting him ready. Then, carrying his schoolbooks, my sister helped him into the car so he wouldn't bump his hands. I moved closer to the window and stared at the golf course. A fine sheen of moisture on the grass reflected the early rays of the sun. The sun rose higher and at last my father walked with an unsteady gait out of the house.

The car croaked as he inserted his key into the ignition. He turned it back off and tried again. "Goddammit!" he muttered and punched the steering wheel when the engine wouldn't kick in.

Ava said cautiously, "Dad, there's no gas."

My father scratched his head in silence. Then he shook his head. "Well, kids, it looks like you're going to have to take the bus today."

Natalie twisted the strap on her books in agitation. "My teacher said she's gonna flunk me if I'm late again."

"Shh," warned Ava getting out of the car.

We piled out after her and crossed the street to the bus stop. My father leaned against the street sign on our corner, watching us as he puffed on a cigarette. After a few moments, the bus appeared a block away.

"Oh no!" Kirk searched inside his gym bag as the bus shrieked to a stop in front of us. "I don't have my other shoe!" It was finals day for the racetrack, and he was pegged to be number one in his class. In her haste to get him ready, Natalie had forgotten to pack both sneakers. "I have to go back and get it!"

"I'll tell the driver to wait!" I called, my eyes on the driver watching us through the open door.

Kirk dropped his bag on the grass and sprinted in front of

the bus. There was a sudden squeal of car brakes and a sickening thud. Natalie sped around the front of the bus with Ava behind her.

"Tell Mom to call an ambulance!" my father bellowed over my sisters' screams as he raced several feet down the road to where my brother lay.

"I'll get her!" Natalie shrieked. She ran across the street, back to our house. "Mom," she yelled as disappeared into the driveway. "You have to get an ambulance!"

A few seconds later, she raced back around the corner to bang on the Rosenbergs' door. My mother was in her nightclothes and told Natalie to get Mrs. Rosenberg to call the ambulance while she got dressed.

I stood frozen at the open door of the bus while Fig doubled over on the curb, crying by himself. A line of cars had stopped in the middle of the road, and my father, bent over Kirk, looked up and shouted that everyone had to keep away.

The bus driver's hands flapped wildly. "He should've never crossed without looking! The car was right there!"

My mother and the ambulance arrived at my brother's side at the same time. Two men climbed out and kneeled beside Kirk to test his reflexes and wrap his head in a white bandage, then hastily bundled him into a blue blanket and loaded him onto a stretcher. As they eased him gently inside the ambulance Kirk's head lolled sideways. The white cloth was soaked in blood. First my mother, then my father climbed up and the ambulance roared off, sirens blaring.

Everyone had vanished. A wailing pierced the thick silence. Holding on to the bus stop for balance leaned an elderly black man weeping in despair. He hadn't seen my brother run into the road until it was too late. His car was jacked up on the grassy curb.

"Don't cry, mister," I said, stroking his sleeve.

He looked down at me, choking on his sobs. "I'm sorry! I didn't mean to hit him. I didn't see, he came out so fast." He fell to his knees. "Jesus, help me!"

I didn't know what to say so I crossed the street and went home.

Two policemen came over that night. My father kept them talking on the doorstep, reassuring them in a low voice that he would think about their advice.

"I'd strongly advise you to prosecute," repeated one of them. "His brakes weren't working."

Natalie pulled her fingers so hard, her knuckles cracked. "It's my fault," she cried. "I should have remembered his sneakers! And now he's going to die!"

"Shut up," scolded Ava. "I'm trying to hear."

My father sounded courteous. "We'll get in touch with you. We can't think about it right now. Thank you for coming."

One of the policemen lit a cigarette before he turned to leave. "Well, you let us know just as soon as you can, Mr. Turner. You can't let them get away with a thing like that."

His colleague pocketed his writing pad and smoothed his hair, nodding.

After he had shut the door firmly behind them, my father cleared his throat and said to my mother, "Don't worry, Lucille, I'm not going to prosecute, just to make sure."

I was too tired to figure out what he meant. I climbed to my room and fell asleep on the bed, still wearing my school clothes.

At breakfast, I asked, "Is the man who hit Kirk going to get in trouble?"

My father gave a start, then his eyes softened with apparent concern. "That poor man. He already has enough problems of his own, why would I want to make them any worse?" He shook his head sadly, as if he believed what he was saying.

Kirk had slipped into a deep coma, and the doctors didn't know if he was going to come out of it. They told my parents that he would either die or be paralyzed for the rest of his life.

"Talking to him might help," my mother was instructed. "Your voice could bring him back."

For the next few weeks, my mother barely left his hospital bedside and talked to him about everything, including the weather, and things, I imagine, that she never told anybody else. With him in a coma, she wouldn't have been scared of being found out.

On the fifteenth day after the accident, when my father was visiting, Kirk suddenly opened his eyes and said, "I'm hungry, Dad." Then he closed his eyes and fell into a natural sleep.

According to my mother, my father got down on his knees and sobbed uncontrollably. I didn't know if it was true. I had never seen him cry.

At first, Kirk couldn't read or write, walk or talk. My mother nursed him back, so that he was able to return to school in a few months and enter the sixth grade, only one grade behind. Perhaps in nursing my brother, she also brought herself back to life.

When my mother was at the hospital teaching Kirk to walk and talk, Natalie stood stiffly on the lawn in a blue dress, arms clinging rakishly to her sides as if letting go would cause her body to collapse like a stack of cards. She sang "Bye Bye Birdie" to herself on the front lawn, wrapped in a pastel green bedspread. My father parked the car halfway down the driveway and stomped into the house.

"Why isn't the table set? Doesn't anyone eat supper around here anymore?"

Natalie shrugged off the bedspread and tiptoed inside. "I'll do it, Dad."

I crept behind her and saw him give her a look of contempt. "What do you mean, you'll do it," he snarled. "Get over here!" He pulled her by the arm and slapped her so hard across the face, her body bounced against the wall.

"Stop it! Dad, stop it!" Ava screamed. She held a spatula in her hand. "Supper's ready!" She banged the spatula against the doorknob, like a dinner bell. "Come on, everybody, sit at the table!"

My father darted toward her, but then a confused look came over his face. He slumped into a chair and buried his face in his hands. We all sat down, not daring to breathe. In the center of the table, Ava placed a bowl of fruit as a treat. A lone banana protruded from the glass bowl, bruised and mushy looking. Natalie remained crouched in her seat all through supper, mechanically shoving food into her mouth.

"Do you know what that those SOBs at the hospital did today?" my father blurted angrily. "Every day they hook up Kirk to a machine to see if he is still alive. Every morning, I have to pay thirty-five dollars before the technician will hook him up. I didn't have the money today."

He blew his nose with a loud honk. "You know what that SOB did when I told him I would pay him later? He started putting the machine away! 'You have to pay me first,' he had the nerve to say."

"What did you do?" Fig asked, wide-eyed.

"Luckily, I bumped into Mr. Rosenberg on the way home. He pulled out his wallet and gave me fifty dollars. I went right back to the hospital and threw it in that technician's face."

"Why don't you have any money?" I asked.

My father's face emptied of expression. "That's a good question," he answered.

Soon after, Natalie's eyes erupted into sores and she had to be taken to the hospital, but not the same one as Kirk because my parents couldn't afford it. The doctor said it was a herpes infection and wanted to keep her in for a few weeks. But it was a charity hospital, and the only place they could put her was in the corridor. My parents brought her home with instructions that she had to lie in the dark until it cleared up.

While Natalie was still confined to her bedroom, Kirk was wheeled into the house by my mother. His face was completely white, and his pajamas hung loosely on his body.

"Hi," he said with a weak smile.

I bent over and hugged him, then wiped his mouth where saliva was spilling out and helped my mother lift him into bed. His hair was short where he had been shaved for his operation, and a thick scar crossed the side of his head. My brother was a shell of his former self, but he was alive. It looked like things were going to get back to normal.

It was summer again and I spent most of the time on the golf course, reading a book. Natalie and Ava hid above the garage listening to the Rolling Stones while my mother read to Kirk on the porch. The bodyguard was gone for good, and it never rained so I didn't have to be scared of getting wet in my room. School was out and my mother said I could go to the beach anytime I wanted, so long as I took some of the kids with me.

Often Fig and Rock would accompany me. The heat of the

sun pouring through the windows of the bus made my back stick to the plastic seat so I stood on my feet, swaying with each turn of the bus. The bus conductor stood in the front, near the open door. Over his cup rose a thin curl of steam.

I went over. "What's that?"

He grinned. "Coffee." He moved aside to let a passenger dismount. "Good day, sir."

I thought for a moment. "How can you drink coffee when it's so hot outside?"

"That's the best time to drink it. Hot liquid makes you sweat and when you sweat, your body cools off."

"Really?"

He laughed. "You didn't know that?"

"My mother won't let us drink coffee," said Fig who'd come up from behind.

"Why, it doesn't have to be coffee, so long as it's hot."

"That's stupid," said Fig. "I don't believe you."

"Well, it's true, young man."

"How do you know it's true?" he argued, sticking his lip out.

"Don't you know adults never lie?" The conductor smiled, tipping back his hat.

"My father says it's okay to lie sometimes," said Fig, looking up at him with serious eyes.

"Shh," I warned, nudging him with my elbow. I smiled at the man. "Just ignore him. He doesn't know what he's talking about."

"Yes I do!" Fig protested, pulling away.

"You should listen to your sister, boy. Anyway, looks like this is your stop. Have fun." He winked at me as we got off the bus.

"'Bye." Clutching Rock firmly by the arm, I waved to the conductor as the bus turned around the corner and disappeared.

"Dad does *so* say it's okay to lie," grumbled Fig, kicking a pebble out of the way. "When he took me to the store, he told the lady we were here on vacation."

"What?" I asked, feeling my stomach jolt.

"Yeah, he said we weren't staying long."

"Rock, get over here! I didn't say you could cross the street yet." I swallowed. "How did you know he was lying?"

"He wasn't lying, stupid. But he said it was okay to tell people we were staying here."

"What are you talking about?"

"Don't you know anything, stupid? We're going back to New York tonight."

"Tonight? That's not true! How do you know?"

"Didn't I tell you Dad told me?"

"Come on, I'm taking you home."

As soon as we arrived back, I threw down my things and ran to my mother in the kitchen. She was making tuna fish sandwiches.

"Mom, are we moving?"

"Your case is already packed and on your bed," she said

blandly. "Go and get it. Then come back and help me with the others' things."

"Why didn't you tell me?" I shouted. "Nobody ever tells me anything!"

"You shut your mouth, young lady. I've got enough problems without you. Now get out of here!"

That night, we left the hurricane state and went back to New York. We were going home with all nine of us intact, in a manner of speaking.

CHAPTER SIX

BACK HOME

My mother said we had spent six months in Mexico and one and a half years each in Nassau, Jacksonville, and Miami Beach. But that added up to five years, and I was only ten when we moved back to New York and seven when we'd left. My parents' untruths thickened and a tightrope appeared, separating the world of truth from the world of lies. I blindly walked this tightrope, never knowing into which abyss I would fall, the one holding the truth or the lies.

Now that we were back in New York, I was to behave as if we had never left. In the last three years, my father had been beaten up and robbed and lost all his money, my mother had tried to kill herself, my brother had almost died, and we'd moved five times. But the bounce in my father's step, the Old Spice, and the freshly laundered handkerchief in his breast pocket made it look like it had all been a dream; a nightmare, not reality.

"Stop looking at me like you don't know where we are," scowled my mother as she unpacked the groceries. "Just go to the park like you always do. And take Marilyn."

I asked Natalie where the park was. She told me to ask the doorman.

We had taken up house on the Upper East Side again, this time on the ninth floor of an apartment building on Seventy-Seventh and Lexington. I shared a room with Marilyn that was so small, there was only room for a bunk bed. I slept on the top and kept forgetting how low the ceiling was, so my day usually started with a bang. Next door was the kitchen, and on the other side, an open-plan living and dining room. Farther down the hallway was Ava and Natalie's room with a small boys' room next door. My parents slept in the master bedroom at the back. The apartment was bare, and my mother had to go out and buy everything new. But she'd lost her flair and covered the apartment in blacks and browns, making it dark and hard to see.

The only remnants of our former life were two photograph albums and a colorized family portrait that my parents had commissioned when I was five. My mother placed this picture of family unity on the wall between my sisters' and brother's bedrooms and it had to be passed on the way to the bathroom. I examined it while waiting my turn, trying to remember what life had been like before we'd left. My mother, smiling with blank eyes, sat firmly in the center with, in these pre-Marilyn days, Rock on her lap. Rock sat bent over, with my mother's white-gloved hands around his waist as his only prop. Kirk lay at her feet and Ava and I stood at one side of her, with Natalie and Fig on the other. My father towered over us all, proud to be the owner of such a large concern. Everyone's mouth was half-open and smiling, except for mine, which was clipped into a thin line, eyes on the photographer in bafflement.

Now that we were back in New York, my father seemed as relaxed and happy as he appeared in the portrait. My mother didn't share his confidence.

"How do you know coming back is a good idea?" she said.

"Why, Lucille, nothing's going to happen."

"How do you know? How can you be sure they're not still looking for you?" There was a rustling behind the closet door as she hung up another dress.

My father lifted his feet onto the bed. "Look, it was three years ago. It must have died down by now. I would have heard something if it hadn't."

My mother tore off the price sticker from her new purse. "You're not planning to get in touch with that family of yours, I hope. That way for sure they'll find you."

My father frowned. "Are you kidding? What do you take me for, a fool?" But from the strain in his voice, it sounded like he had been considering it.

"Hmm." My mother cleared her throat with a grating sound. "Well, just don't be doing anything stupid. It would be nice if we could stay in one place for a while. All this packing and unpacking is getting on my nerves."

My father sounded annoyed. "I said to get someone to help you."

"Oh yeah?" My mother snorted. "And where was I supposed to get the money?"

"Look, I told you. That's over now. Things are back the way they were."

"Jeez, that's a relief." My mother turned her back. "Just don't go buying me any mink coats this time."

My father sounded surprised. "What are you talking about?"

"You know very well what I'm talking about. I'd rather you didn't give me any presents if you're going to end up selling them. Whenever you said pack up, I thought it was for storage."

So, I thought, creeping away from the door, that's why we never arrived with anything.

Next to my parents' room, on the way back to the living room, was a hallway closet crammed full of suitcases, cleaners, and rags. On the top, reachable by a footstool, was a Bustelo coffee can filled with small change for the laundry. So many of us stole from the can, I was surprised my parents never found out that money was missing. It was hard not to notice, though, when it came to the top drawer of their bedroom dresser. It was a wooden drawer, long and flat and filled with jewelry, perfume samplers, lipstick, tissues, dollar bills, and small change.

One night at supper, my father asked, "Who's been taking money from my drawer?"

There was a long silence. I felt like I was choking and didn't dare look at anyone, frightened that he would search under my mattress and find the handful of bills I had snatched from the bureau. My father seemed to grow larger, looming at the head of the table like a dark vapor.

"I have to go to the bathroom," I mumbled, and slipped away from the table. I grabbed the money from my bed and raced down the hallway to my parents' room, just out of sight of the dinner table. After shoving the money back into the drawer, I flushed the toilet a couple of times as a disguise, then slipped back into my seat.

"Wow," I said, picking up my napkin. "I was bursting."

At the end of the meal, my father detained me. "I want to talk to you," he said, and motioned for me to follow him into the living room. He removed a cigarette from his gold case, tapped it two, three, four times and inserted it into his black cigarette holder. He glanced at me every so often, seeming to enjoy my terror. Smoke rings blew out of his mouth, and he casually watched them disappear into the air.

"Have you been taking money?"

"No, Dad."

"Don't lie to me. I have a way of telling, you know. Even when you think you're being smart, I can see what you're do-ing." My father smiled. "You're too young to know this, but I've always been able to keep out of trouble because I can tell what people are thinking. How do you think I've been able to look after all of you so well?" He paused. "I'll give you one more chance. Did you take the money?"

I tried to keep my eyes steady, willing my heart to stop bouncing me against the chair. "Honest, I didn't."

Later that night, as I lay in bed with a sore backside, I stared at the ceiling, wondering how he had found out that it was me who had taken the money. I was sure he hadn't noticed me leave the table—how could he know I was the one? I felt like he was looking at me through the wall, filling my head with his stare, reading the crevices of my mind. It was like he had some strange, mystical power of being everywhere at once. I was an atheist—my parents had told me so—but I knew without a doubt that my father was God.

Two weeks after we returned to New York, I started sixth grade. At the commencement of class, Mr. Fleischmann ordered the students to raise our left hands when answering roll call. I wasn't used to being near the beginning of the alphabet, and when it was my turn to answer, I was caught undoing one of my cuffs. Mr. Fleischmann tapped his foot impatiently.

"Tosca Auster! Are you with us?"

"Wait a second," I called, rolling up my sleeves.

Mr. Fleischmann frowned. "Put your hand up this instant!"

"Wait," I said again. "I'm just looking."

"Stop looking and answer me!" he bellowed.

"I can't until I find the mole."

"What in god's name are you talking about?" He looked across at me, furious.

"You know, the mole. The one on your left arm." I hadn't

realized that the mole was not something everyone had to distinguish left from right.

"What a silly girl." He shook his head scornfully.

I flushed. "I am not silly."

"What did you say?"

"Nothing."

After that, Mr. Fleischmann treated me as if I annoyed him on purpose. So I did. I mimicked him behind his back and laughed in his face when he caught me. Knowing how much neatness meant to him, I handed in homework on crumpled pieces of paper. I waved my hand in the air and then told him I forgot when he called on me. I wrote swear words in the margins of our textbooks and threw chalk out the window during recess.

Mr. Fleischmann paid me back for my insurgency. He ignored me when I put up my hand, then graded me poorly for not participating in class. He laughed when he heard the kids call me Nose. Out of the blue, he ordered us to lift the tops of our desks so he could see inside, shrieking in horror when he saw mine filled with bunched-up candy wrappers. He didn't care that there were large gaps in my learning because I had moved so much, or that my father expected me to get good grades but often wasn't there to read the report cards. He didn't ask why I was so easily distracted, or why I sometimes arrived with eyes red from crying because my father or mother had hit me.

Kirk was well enough to go back to school, but because he

had missed so much, was put into my class. My parents said he was normal and he acted like he was. Except for the lisp that went away after a while, his shaky memory and not being athletic anymore, he was as good as new. True, his speech was sometimes slurred and he was often slow on the uptake, but so what. My parents pretended the accident had never happened, and therefore so did we.

Kirk and I didn't sit next to each other—the boys were at one end of the class and the girls at the other. My neighbor was Nickie Stein. She had long blonde hair and a dimple in her cheek. Nickie had to sit in the front row because she'd been caught trying to hide her bubble gum on the light switch while waiting for her seat assignment on the first day.

"What a jerk," she whispered as Mr. Fleischmann passed our desk on his way to making us recite the Pledge of Allegiance. She lay her hand flat next to mine. "Give me five."

I looked at her, eyebrows raised. She motioned for me to place my hand over hers and slap it.

"What does that mean?"

She snorted derisively. "Everybody knows that!"

"Well, just because I don't doesn't mean you can laugh at me." I glared at her.

"Okay, class, on your feet!" boomed Mr. Fleischmann.

"I pledge allegiance to the flag . . ." I knew the words as I'd had to say them every morning in Miami Beach. At the other end of the classroom, Kirk looked confused. His hand lay on his heart, not like the other boys who were saluting, and his mouth hung open. I tried to catch his attention with a hissing sound, but he continued to stare blankly at the flag.

Nickie nudged me and mouthed, "Get a load of that moron."

I could feel my face reddening. "That's my brother!"

"What's wrong with him?"

I didn't answer. It was none of her business—as my mother would say.

Because we were in the same class and had the same friends, Kirk and I became as close as a sister and a brother could in a family such as ours. His nickname was Girl and mine was Fatty. It started with my mother telling me that if I didn't sit down when I ate, I'd get fat legs because all the food would lodge there.

"Ha-ha," chuckled Kirk. "Fatty."

"Well, you're just a girl. Everyone says so."

My mother slapped me. "Don't call him that, you hear?"

"He called me Fatty," I protested.

"Will you cut it out and eat your lunch? And sit down."

When the school went on a Halloween UNICEF drive, Kirk and I combined forces and stood outside our building collecting money. We were taught that American Indians were savages, so we thought it was funny for Kirk to smear lipstick on his face and whoop at people to put money in our can. I stood by his side, parading as a housewife in a nightgown and rollers. Anyone who made the mistake of passing our corner was pestered so much that we ended up with fifty-five dollars, more than all the other kids at school. It helped that we stayed outside from eight o'clock in the morning to six o'clock at night, not letting up for an instant with our pleas to save the children. No one could see the bruises on my ribs from my mother's rage the night before.

I had been lying on the floor in the living room, listening to Simon and Garfunkel on the radio. "Hello darkness my old friend . . ."

My mother shouted my name from the kitchen. It was suppertime and I was supposed to be setting the table.

"I've come to talk with you again . . ."

I pretended I couldn't hear and turned the knob louder.

"softly creeping . . . while I was sleeping . . ."

I felt a blow on my ribs.

"Get up! Get up, I said!" She kicked me again. I rolled away to protect myself.

"Mom!" I cried.

"You shut the hell up! What do you think I am? Your maid? Get off the floor!" She picked up an ashtray and threw it at me. I ducked and it landed on the radio, shattering its face.

"Mom!" shouted Natalie.

My mother spun around. "Don't you start, young lady! You get back to that kitchen!"

She swiveled back, but I had already crawled into the dining room. At least my father wasn't home to make it worse.

––––––

Nickie lived in an apartment building four blocks away, on a street lined with trees. A cold wind blew red and gold leaves across the concrete pavement as I shuffled my feet on the way to her house, loving the crackling sound they made.

Nickie's building was brick, too, but she didn't have a doorman. Her mother wore a white apron as she cooked in the kitchen. She'd swept her auburn hair into a bun, but several strands had broken free and lay on her neck.

"Hi, sweetheart, how was your day?" she asked, kissing Nickie on the cheek.

Nickie threw her books on the table and poked a finger into the cake mix. "Okay. Mom, this is Tosca. She just moved here."

"Oh?" Mrs. Stein raised her eyebrows. "Where from?"

I paused, trying to think of what to say. "Um, well, we used to live in New York." That seemed the safest way to put it.

Mrs. Stein smiled. "Are you glad you're back?" I smelled a mixture of toast and perfume as she crossed over to pat my head.

"Yeah. I like it here." I held my forefinger greedily over the enamel bowl. "Can I have some, too?"

"Of course you can, honey. Here, let me get you a spoon so you can have a nice dollop. There. Now go and play so I'll have enough left for the cake."

"My father's a musician," said Nickie, showing me the stacks of music in the piano stool. "He plays in an orchestra."

I remembered Mr. Oldstein, the piano teacher we'd had when we lived on York Avenue. "I used to play piano," I said.

"What happened?"

I shrugged. "I don't know. I guess my parents don't like the piano anymore. Do you have any records?"

"Duh!"

In Nickie's room were so many records and dolls and books, there was hardly any room to sit down. "My mother keeps telling me she's going to give them away, but she doesn't mean it."

Mrs. Stein poked her head in the door. "Want some soup, girls?"

I nodded and followed her back to the kitchen. She handed me a bowl of thin yellow liquid with a large ball in the middle. "What's that?"

"You don't know what that is? Why, that's chicken and matzo ball soup." Mrs. Stein turned to me and wrinkled her brow. "But I thought you were Jewish."

I put up my head eagerly. "No, I'm an atheist," I said, reaching for a spoon.

Mrs. Stein laughed. "I wouldn't exactly say we are religious ourselves, but being Jewish is more than that, you know. Where are your folks from?" When I didn't answer, she said, "Your parents." She leaned over and ruffled my hair, like she thought I was cute.

I felt myself blush. "Um, they're from New York."

"How about your grandparents? Nickie's Grandma Goldie comes from Poland, doesn't she, Nickie? She hated that place, filthy pigs."

"Uh-huh," Nickie mumbled through her matzo ball.

I felt funny. I could barely remember my grandmother, the

wrinkled old lady with gray hair who smelled like mothballs and chocolate raisins.

"I think they're dead." I felt sweat break out on my neck.

"Oh, that's a shame," she said, patting my shoulder. She leaned back against the counter and squinted at me. "Everyone has to come from somewhere. Where were your mother's parents from?"

"I don't know. England, I think."

She looked puzzled. "England? Well, they could have been Jewish. There's plenty of Jews there. There's even Jews in Italy, you know, even though people think they're all Catholic over there."

She put her finger to her lips and rubbed them for a moment, smearing her lipstick slightly at the corner of her mouth. "Auster. That could have been shortened at Ellis Island, maybe Austerlitz or something?"

I kept my head down and continued spooning up the soup.

But the next morning at breakfast, I asked my father, "Dad, where was Grandma from?"

"Russia," he said, not looking up from the newspaper.

"Was she Jewish?"

His paper rustled slightly. "No," he said. His clear blue eyes appeared briefly over the paper. "She was Catholic." He paused. "I think."

I told Mrs. Stein the next time I was at Nickie's house.

"Well, that explains it then," she said. But she still looked at me funny with her hands resting on her apron.

After that, Nickie brought me half-sour pickles for lunch. In exchange, I brought her peanut butter and jelly sandwiches that I made behind my mother's back. I knew my mother would be mad if she saw me taking food for someone else.

"What do you want her over for? Doesn't she have her own home where she can eat?" my mother said when I'd asked if Nickie could come over for supper.

"But Mom, every time I go to her house, her mother gives me food. I want to pay her back."

My mother sighed. "Look, I have enough kids to feed. Don't bother me." She tapped her nails against the counter. "And don't go over there. I don't want you eating at anyone's house."

"Why not?" I wished I hadn't said anything.

"Just do as I say."

But I still went over to Nickie's house after school. I told my mother I had joined a basketball team. She didn't realize I hardly knew how to throw a ball, let alone get one through a hoop.

Our neighbor from upstairs knocked on our door and asked if I could take her daughter, Marilyn's friend, Alison, to the park. Mrs. Simpson was all sharp corners, topped by a stiff, triangular smile.

"I'll give you two dollars," she said. "Bring her back at five."

When I told my mother, she said brightly, "Wow, a whole two dollars. I'd have you take Marilyn, but she's sleeping. Lucky you."

I lifted Alison. "Come on, let's go." With the little girl clutched tightly against my chest, I felt warm inside.

"Let me down. I wanna walk." Alison struggled out of my arms, and under a crystal blue sky, we proceeded to the pond in Central Park, a few blocks away. A spring breeze blew, clearing away the dank gray of winter, and once again, the trees had come alive and made the streets look fresh and green. But it was still cold, and I blew on my fingers to keep warm. I planted myself on a bench and watched Alison play with a little boy on the steps leading into the water. A girl walked by eating a large pretzel, looking strangely familiar. She stared back at me.

"Hey, aren't you Tosca Ring's sister?"

I gave a start and looked around quickly to see if anyone had heard.

"No, I'm Tosca. Who are you?" Hearing my old name sent a shudder of pleasure through me, tinged with a sense of disloyalty.

"Donna Cohen. Don't you remember? I used to sit next to you at school." She licked salt crumbs from her mouth.

"Donna?" I frowned. Her thin, oval face surrounded by straight brown hair looked vaguely familiar, but it was the slightly crooked angle of her eyes that jarred my memory. Donna and I had been the only ones who hadn't cried on the first day of elementary school. My father had dropped me off, saying, "Be a big girl." All the other kids and their parents had been crying and screaming. Donna and I had thought we were more grown up than everyone else and that had given us a good enough reason to become friends.

"You look just like your sister," she giggled now.

I felt shaky. "Where do you live?" I asked in a rush. "Can I have your telephone number? Can I come to your house?"

"Sure, I'll ask my mother," she said casually, as if it were the most natural thing in the world. "What happened to you?"

"We moved." I changed the subject. "I live on Seventy-Seventh Street. Where do you live?"

Before she could answer, a woman came and tapped me on the shoulder. "Hey, aren't you looking after that little girl?"

I looked over to see Alison's head vanishing into the pond. "Christ!" I sprang over and yanked her out. She burst into tears. "Wet! All wet!"

"I'm gonna get killed!" I cried.

"Don't worry. We can dry her off." Donna pulled up her sleeves. "Stop crying!" she scolded Alison as she wiped her down.

Alison was still covered in sludge by the time we reached the exit. "I have to go this way," said Donna, pointing up Fifth Avenue. "Here," and she thrust her phone number at me. "'Bye."

I stared after her. Then I picked up Alison and took her home.

The Simpsons' housekeeper screamed when she opened the door. She pulled Alison inside and waved me away. "You'd better go home. I'll take care of this."

While we ate supper, the doorbell rang and Mrs. Simpson appeared. She barged in toward me with her finger stabbing the air. "You almost murdered my daughter!"

I gulped.

"What happened?" said my father, wiping his mouth with a napkin.

"That daughter of yours almost drowned my little girl in the lake," Mrs. Simpson said through gritted teeth.

"Well, that's not so bad," said my father cheerfully. "She didn't drown, did she?"

Mrs. Simpson gasped. "Well! Some family this is!"

My father turned red. "Let me show you the door, Mrs. What-did-you-say-your-name-was?"

"That's right, you tell her," whispered Fig, punching the air with his fists.

"Can I have my two dollars?" I asked.

Mrs. Simpson made a sound like something inside her had popped and slammed the door.

"Idiot," muttered my mother. "I'll give you the two dollars. Just don't go over there again."

When my mother overheard me telling Natalie I'd run into Donna at the park, she took her number from me and tore it into little pieces. "You're not calling anyone unless I say so," she said. "Forget about her."

I tried to remember what the number was and even looked it up in the phone book, but there were five pages of Cohens so I gave up.

———

Ava and Natalie's room was covered in posters of Sonny and Cher, the Mamas and the Papas, and the Lovin' Spoonful. They kept their door shut most of the time, hooting with laughter. Ava went to Julia Richmond High School where the girls acted tough and took drugs in the bathroom. She ironed the frizz out of her hair, drew thick black lines around her eyes, and dressed in pants that hugged her thighs but had such wide bottoms an elephant could have lived in them. She was trying to look like Cher. After school, telling my mother she was doing her homework in the library where it was nice and quiet, she went down to the Village and smoked reefers. She let Natalie go with her sometimes but never me, saying I was too young. Natalie came back from her sojourns and showed me how to walk barefoot on the streets and puff cigarettes.

One day, Natalie decided to curl her hair and we went down to the drugstore. After hiding a packet of rollers under her shirt, she and I slipped into the supermarket next door for cookies. We loitered in the aisle, trying to choose between chocolate-covereds or creme-filleds or just plains against a background of muzak. Three tunes later, we still couldn't decide.

"Let's get out of here," said Natalie. Blinded by the sun, I didn't catch on at first that a man had followed us out and was propelling my sister back inside the store.

"Tosca, help!" she screamed, trying to free herself.

"Wait! Wait! She didn't do anything!" I yelled, trying to grab his arm.

The man pinned her against the checkout counter like she was a criminal.

"Mister, please leave my sister alone," I pleaded. "She didn't do anything."

"Show me what you have under your shirt," he commanded her.

"Nothing," Natalie declared. But when the man attempted to touch her, she reached for the rollers with shaking fingers.

"You stole these, didn't you?"

"No. Honest."

"Where did you get them, then?"

"At the drugstore."

"Show me the receipt."

"I threw it away."

"Yeah, sure. Andy," he called to the stocker. "Check on the shelves to see if we carry these rollers." He shook Natalie. "If you got these here, you're in for a lot of trouble, young lady."

Luckily for us, no matter how much the boy searched the shelves, he couldn't find the brand. The man had to let us go.

"Don't let me catch you in here again," he said with a nasty scowl.

Natalie was walking funny, but I didn't notice anything until she asked me to look at the seat of her pants when we were in the elevator in our building. A big patch of wetness circled her pants where she'd peed herself. The shame on her face made me feel like crying. I tried to reassure her it didn't matter, the man was a jerk. But I made myself a silent promise never to let anyone make me feel like that, not my father, not anyone.

Soon after, on my way to the YMCA with Nickie, a group of eight schoolgirls apprehended us halfway up the hill.

One of them pushed her face into mine. "What school do you go to?"

"P.S. 190," I smiled, thinking she wanted to make friends. Nickie became catatonic and flattened herself against the wall.

"Oh, yeah?" rejoined another girl. "We don't like girls from that school."

"Yeah," said a third, and shoved me into the street. I tried to push back, but they were too much competition for my non-athletic body. A car honked loudly as I fell over in the street. Angry and frightened, I gathered as much steam as I could and bellowed, "Fuck off!" Then I froze, expecting to be pummeled to death. To my astonishment, the force of my yell must have surprised the hell out of them because all of a sudden where there were eight, there were none. Nickie looked at me in awe and I savored my victory, feeling for the first time a sense of the power that would later prove to inflame my parents beyond all reason.

Ava was learning her own strength at the same time and flexing it at home. Only last week, when she'd brought her boyfriend home, she'd cried epithets no one had dared utter in our house.

Ava's boyfriend was called Marcel. I walked in on them as they kissed on her bed.

"Get the hell out of here," said Ava, kicking the door shut.

When my mother got home from shopping, they were playing Scrabble in the living room. I hid behind the couch, hoping they would kiss again so I could watch.

"Can I please use the phone, Mrs. Auster?" asked Marcel. "I have to call my mother to tell her when I'll be back."

"Maybe you should go now," said my mother. "Before my husband comes home."

Ava motioned to him to ignore her, and he picked up the telephone and dialed. My mother frowned but continued emptying grocery bags. A key turned in the lock.

I shrank against the wall and waited.

Oblivious, Marcel spoke quietly into the phone, then laughed and hung up. When he turned around, my father was facing him. Marcel gave a start, then grinned and held out a hand. "Hello, Mr. Auster. I'm Marcel, a friend of Ava's."

"I think you'd better leave, Marcel," said my father in a quiet voice. "Let me show you the door."

"Dad!" protested Ava. My father pushed her out of the way and banged the front door shut on Marcel. My sister faced him defiantly. "Why did you do that?"

"Go to your room!"

"I will not go to my room! I'm not a kid anymore! Why did you throw my friend out? He's my friend. You have no right to do that!"

My father raised his arm. "Get to your room!" he shouted.
"No!"

His fist flew through the air and knocked her down. Ava remained still for a moment, then jumped to her feet. "Don't you fucking hit me!" My father punched her again and she crashed into the wall.

My mother leaned against the kitchen doorway, waving a bread knife. "How dare you talk to your father like that!"

I shrank flatly against the family picture.

"I'll go when I fucking well want, you shithead," my sister screeched. She spun around and ran into her room.

When my father came home the next day, the family portrait was stuck full of pins. My father exploded into my sisters' room while they were reading on their beds. He brandished a ruler.

"You want to destroy pictures? I'll show you how to destroy pictures!" He scraped the end of the ruler back and forth against the walls until all the posters were ripped and on the floor. "That'll show you!" He swiveled on his well-polished heels and hurled the door so hard, the building shook.

I heard Ava laugh loudly through the door, "That'll show *you*, asshole!"

Natalie said my father kicked Marcel out because he was black. I was confused. I thought my father liked black people. When we lived in Jacksonville, my father had agreed with Natalie that it was unfair we weren't allowed to go to the same schools as black kids. "They have been denied their civil rights for too long!" he exclaimed. And later, after the accident in Miami Beach, he didn't prosecute the man who had run over Kirk, saying the poor man had enough problems already. He had shaken his head sadly, like he meant it.

Natalie also had a boyfriend. His name was Lewis, but she was smart enough not to bring him home. He was black, too. I saw them on the corner on the way back from school. As he and my sister kissed he held her loosely around the back, as if to protect her from falling. I watched for a while from under the canopy of the building, then went up and touched her on the arm.

"Better hurry. Dad's going to be home soon."

"Hey, Lewis, this is my sister, Tosca."

Lewis turned around and smiled. "Hi, Tosca."

"Hi," I replied. "Come on, Nat. Dad's going to kill you if he sees you."

"He can get fucked," said my sister with her head thrown back, but I could see from her eyes she was scared. "See you tomorrow, Lewis." They kissed again and she followed me into the building.

"I hate Dad," she muttered.

"So do I." But I didn't. I just wanted him to be different.

ell no, we won't go!"

"What do we say?"

"Hell *no*, we won't *go*!"

I raced to catch up with the crowd that was yelling about the Vietnam War. I tripped by long-haired mothers with babies, men with red bandanas tied around their foreheads, old women with canes and men in worn uniforms, children carrying placards that read Peace and teenagers with long hair and bare feet and buttons declaring Make Love Not War. The shouting grew louder as the marchers strode quickly toward Fifty-Ninth Street. The sun poured down, filling the air with the musky smell of cherry blossom that rose along the brown walls of the park.

"Reds!" "Commie traitors!" A bunch of oranges came hurtling through the air. The people lining Fifth Avenue wore plaid shirts and baseball caps. They raised their fists as they jeered at us.

"Losers!" shouted a woman covered in buttons next to me. "If you like war so much, why don't you go and leave our men here?" She ducked, and an orange landed at her feet.

"Communist sympathizer! Why don't you go back to Russia where you belong?"

Russia. The word sounded romantic, exciting. That was where my parents had tried to go when my father was a Communist. It wasn't their fault they were denied visas. It made me feel part of something, doing the same thing my parents had done in the same place they had done it—and with people who were just like us.

"Hey Natalie," I shouted. "Do you think Mom and Dad did this? When they were young?"

Natalie moved fast, but she turned around and shouted back, "I don't know!"

As I jogged to keep up with her I scanned the crowd on the sidelines. The bystanders' faces were red with fury and their arms full of hate. Laughing in their faces, the demonstrators threw the oranges back. If this was Communism, I thought, picking up an orange to hurl it back, it was fun.

June marked the end of elementary school for Kirk and me. One of the kids in our class had a graduation party.

"Come on, let's play Spin the Bottle," said Nickie.

We sat on the floor in a circle. When it was my turn, the bottle pointed at Billy, Kirk's best friend. He was half-Japanese and half-American and once brought my brother and me to his project on One Hundred and Third Street. We played catch in the concrete courtyard, then went upstairs to his apartment. The living room was stuffed with dark green furniture and photographs of a man in an army uniform. In the large one on the wall, the man's head was cocked to one side as he smiled broadly.

Billy's mother appeared in a kimono and house slippers and brought us tea as we arranged ourselves politely on the sofa. She sat with us, smiling, telling us that she had met her husband in the war.

"He was a good man," she said, wiping the picture frame with a napkin. "Not like those other Americans who locked up my people in this country." Her eyes grew sharp, and she banged down her cup. Tea slopped into the saucer. I looked at Kirk with my eyebrows raised.

"Those people have a lot to pay for," she said bitterly, twisting a piece of hair behind her ear.

Later, at school, I asked Billy what she meant.

"They locked up Japanese people during the war."

"What for?"

He shrugged. "I don't know."

Then I said, hesitantly, "Did they kill your father?"

"No, stupid," he said. "They only did it to the Japanese."

I felt like a fool so I said belligerently, "So how did he die then, if you're so smart?"

He turned away. "In a car accident." He pushed me out of his way and ran down the stairs.

At the party, he pressed his lips to mine, blushing. He seemed to have forgotten how stupid I was. I kept my mouth tightly shut and held my breath. He tried to pull away, but I wouldn't let him, not until there was no breath left and everything was turning white.

"Hey! Hey!" shouted Nickie. "It's my turn." The bottle landed at Kirk's place, but he refused to kiss her.

"Come on, I want to write in the autograph albums," he said, standing up.

So we exchanged our books and wrote our addresses and good luck wishes for our graduation into junior high school. In mine were poems like "Roses are red, violets are blue, I have a nose, but you have a bigger one too" and others merely saying

"Good luck in junior high school." Nickie wrote, "You'll always be my best friend. I love you." In hers, I inscribed inside a heart, "Friends forever."

Then we went back to being kids and threw chairs at one another. Billy chased Nickie and me into the hallway and we tore into the elevator, screaming wildly as we sped up and down, preventing anyone else in the building from getting in.

The night of Ava's last day of the school year, she was picked up by the police on the subway. She and Marcel had fallen into a stupor from a cocktail of red wine and sleeping pills and were rolling around on the floor of a subway car on their way to Coney Island. My mother had to pick her up in the hospital, where the drugs were pumped out of her stomach, and drag her home. Woken by the commotion, Natalie and I stood by the bathroom door and watched as our sister threw up purple in the bathtub. My mother muttered angrily to herself while she cleaned up, saying Ava should count herself lucky my father was out of town, but just as soon as he came back, boy would she be in for it.

My father hadn't been home for a while. Through compressed lips, my mother had said he was away on business. At first, I thought she was mad at him for not taking her again. "I didn't get married to be stuck on my own with a bunch of kids," she'd yelled the last time he left. But this time he wasn't on a business trip, he was somewhere else, somewhere my mother wouldn't tell us. The day before Ava was picked up, a man in a gray suit had come over. My mother shooed us out of the living room.

He spoke in a low voice. "It's pretty serious," he said. "They're refusing to let him out until next week."

"But, Frank, how did they find him?" my mother whispered in a trembling voice.

"Someone recognized him. They picked him up on the street, just outside the restaurant. At the station, they only let him make one phone call."

The man paused to take some papers from his briefcase. "But there is something we can do. If you can testify in court on Monday, that'll help a lot. We'll at least get him out on bail and try to have the trial delayed for a few weeks. It shouldn't be set at more than fifty thousand dollars if we're lucky. All you have to do is say what I tell you, okay?"

My mother nodded, twisting her wedding ring back and forth.

"If the prosecuting attorney asks you why you moved, say it was because of your health. They're not going to know any different. And certainly do not say anything about the bank accounts."

"What bank accounts?" my mother asked.

"The ones set up under pseudonyms. Didn't he tell you?"

Natalie, Ava, and I had a conference of our own that night after my mother had gone to bed.

"I don't care what happens to him," Ava said angrily, "so long as we don't have to move. He can go to hell for all I care."

"What are they going to do to him?" Fear gripped my stomach.

Natalie nodded anxiously. "Mom's going to be mad all the time. What if she doesn't let us go out?"

Ava laughed. "Let's just tell her we have to do stuff at school. She'll never know the difference."

On Monday, my mother left the house early, lying that she was going to have her hair done rather than admitting she'd be testifying for my father in court. The same night, my father came back, looking tired and disheveled and smelling bad. The next morning, when he was all washed and shaved again, he called us together and informed us we were going to Scotland on vacation.

"I don't believe you," said Ava. "You're making us move again."

"I am not." My father frowned. "Whatever makes you think that?"

Ava stamped her foot. "If you make us stay there, I'm coming back."

My father sighed heavily as if she was just being troublesome. "I mean it. It's just a vacation."

"I mean it, too, Dad. I'm coming back. I'm sixteen. I can do what I like." Underneath her show of bravado, Ava looked frightened.

It was sticky hot. With sweat pouring down my back, I observed Ava and my father arguing and my mother mechanically dragging one suitcase after another from the hallway closet. I called Nickie.

"Send me a postcard," she said. "I'll paste it on my wall."

"Okay," I said. "I wish you could come, too."

"Hold on, my mother wants to say something."

"Hello, sweetie. You take care and come back safe. Maybe your mother will let you come upstate on Labor Day, okay?"

"Okay, Mrs. Stein. 'Bye."

My mother helped us pack for the warmth and cold, saying, "You never know what the weather's going to be like," and we left the next day.

I didn't look back at the tall buildings, the white smoke of the subway rising in the street like soft clouds, at the corner stands fragrant with hot dogs and sauerkraut, or at the sun shining down on people who looked and talked like me and my family. My father said we were coming back, and I believed him.

CHAPTER SEVEN

OCH AYE THE NOO

On our way from the airport to Ayr in Scotland where we were to spend our vacation, the taxi driver stopped the car at the top of a hill and told us to look below.

"Och, isn't it bonny," he said, and even though I didn't understand what he had said, I knew he meant for us to admire his country.

I looked down at the gray dampness and thought how ugly it was. The sky was so low, it seemed indistinguishable from the stark hills of the Scottish Lowlands. At my feet lay rows of stone houses and rain-streaked roads. Bright purple sprigs of heather provided the only relief from the unremitting dreariness.

"That's our national flower," said the driver.

"Are we there yet?" I asked, shuddering with cold.

The driver laughed. "Ay, wee lassie, you'll nae be lang hame."

"What?"

He chuckled. "You'll know soon enough."

On the airplane, my mother had browsed a brochure on

which were illustrated yellow-haired men and women dressed in blue coats, smiling against a background of sun and sea.

"This is where we're going," she said. "It's called Dougalls Holiday Camp."

"What's a holiday camp?" Fig had yawned.

"It's a place where families stay on vacation." My mother's voice was quick, high, cheerful, like a balloon let off in the air. "They have a swimming pool, a dance hall, oh, all kinds of things. It's organized so you know what you're doing."

"Why do we need people to organize us?" I asked.

"Don't start that again," she answered crossly.

"Is there a roller coaster?" asked Rock.

Puckering her lips, my mother opened her compact. "Stop being so spoiled."

Dougalls turned out to be the exact opposite of what the brochure had promised. Built like a small town, streets divided chalets in neat lines, much like a prison camp. Loudspeakers were placed strategically throughout the area, and every morning a bugle would go off, followed by a gleeful "Good Morning Campers," our signal that sleep was now verboten.

Struggling out of bed in the cold damp of the small one-room cottages, I stuffed my body into jeans and headed with the crowds toward the huge mess hall. We stood in lines clutching tin trays with hundreds of others and were doled out rubbery scrambled eggs and little sausages, cornflakes, and a cup of tea. Glancing secretly at my mother before moving to the sugar bowl, I scooped large tablespoonfuls onto everything.

One half hour was allowed for breakfast, enough time to get into a fight or watch my parents' blank faces with puzzlement. Then we were off to group activities—swimming, calisthenics, bingo, or sing-alongs. The activities were the camp's attempt to make people forget their troubles. At least, that's what the brochure had said, spelling "trouble" with a capital *T*. It reminded me of a joke my father used to tell. There were two brothers, Trouble and Shut Up. One day, they were playing hide-and-seek and Shut Up couldn't find Trouble anywhere. He saw a policeman and asked, "Hey, have you seen my brother?"

"Why, what's your name, little boy?"

"Shut Up," he answered.

The policeman shook his fist. "Are you looking for Trouble?"

"Yeah, how did you know?" said Shut Up.

But there hadn't been any jokes for a while, or having to laugh when it wasn't funny.

Natalie and I snuck away as often as we could to steal chocolate and smoke cigarettes, getting into Trouble of our own. I couldn't understand what anyone said. But it didn't matter. We found some cans of beer at the back of the mess hall and got so drunk we didn't care if we could understand anyone or not. Then we got hold of a tube of glue and tried to get high in the bathroom, which was a row of stone stalls, cold and gloomy. Maybe we didn't hold the paper bag correctly, but after rolling around for a few minutes pretending to be stoned, we gave up and went back to roaming between the chalets.

The people at the camp had cheeks rubbed raw by the wind,

watery, red-rimmed eyes, sandy hair that was singularly straight and often stringy, and short, stubby noses. Everyone spoke English, however unintelligible, giving the impression we had something in common. But it was an illusion, and I must have seemed as foreign to them as they seemed to me. It was as if none of us knew where to place one another. The air was laced with an iciness blown in fresh from the Atlantic, but everyone wore bathing suits because it was summer. No doubt on June twenty-first, the loudspeakers had blared an order for everyone to take off their clothes.

A beefy, orange-haired man, also there on vacation, offered to take Natalie and me into town in a taxi. He sat in the back between us and put his arm around me so his hand cupped my breast. I squeezed my arm tightly against my side to make him move it, but he only gripped harder. When we got back to our cottage, I sat on the windowsill and cried. He'd made me feel dirty and ugly, and I wanted to go back home.

A man carrying a briefcase came to visit us one day while we were in one of the chalets fighting over Scrabble.

"Hello, my name's Mr. McKenzie," he boomed cheerfully. "Is your father here?"

"I'll get him," said Kirk officiously.

"What do you want to see him about?" I asked.

Mr. McKenzie laughed, showing uneven, tea-stained teeth

beneath his mustache. "He's going to be working with me. Didn't he tell you? He's going to help me market Scotch. I sponsored him so he can work here." He pulled out a pipe and stuffed it with strong-smelling tobacco. "He's a smart man, your father. I'm lucky he wanted to come all this way."

"Lucky," echoed Natalie, looking out the window at the fog blowing in from the sea.

"How long have you known him?" I asked, trying to keep the curiosity from my voice.

Mr. McKenzie smiled broadly. "I must have met him when some of you were just a twinkling in your mother's eye." He stroked his jaw thoughtfully. "It's the funniest thing. I was sure his name was Ring, but all these years, I had the spelling wrong."

"Why, what is it?" asked Fig quickly. Natalie looked at him, warning him to be quiet.

"Why, you look old enough to know your own last name, laddie. It's Rung, Master Rung. What's your first name?"

But then my father came in smiling, hand outstretched. The slant of his tie showed he had dressed quickly. As always, a handkerchief sat upright in the breast pocket of his jacket.

"Hello, I see you've met my children. Come this way. I know a place where we can talk."

When they had gone, Kirk pulled his eyebrows in vexation. "I thought he said we were here on vacation."

Ava inhaled sharply. "We'd better be here on vacation."

Natalie clutched her hands, a look of fear sweeping across

her face. "Of course we are. They would have told us by now if we had to stay."

Ava frowned. "You'd better be right."

As my parents had promised, we did stay at Dougalls for three weeks, and I counted off the days on my fingers. When it was time to leave, my father took us for a drive to nearby Glasgow, a city twenty-five miles from the coast. Bulbous black clouds refusing to either pour rain or go away hung dismally in the sky as we turned into a street lined with houses.

After pulling into a gray-pebbled driveway, my father said, "Welcome to your new home, kids."

I felt like I'd been punched in the stomach. "But why do we have to move again?" I asked feebly as my mother walked to the front door with a key in hand.

"I knew it!" Ava burst into tears and jumped out of the car. Paralyzed, Natalie stared blankly at the house.

My father said calmly, "It's for your own welfare. You know as well as I do how bad things have been getting in the States. The schools . . ." He gestured toward Ava. "The Vietnam War . . ." He nodded at my brothers.

My arms felt lifeless as I unpacked my case. Numbly, I sat on the floor of my new bedroom and paged through my autograph album squeezed into the bottom, unfolding the triangles of colored paper to read what my friends had left for me.

———

Glasgow. Old, cold, grimy. Separated into rich and poor sections, its outskirts were littered with crumbling government-subsidized housing with graffiti covering the walls, "Tongs ya bass, Partick ya bass," gangs declaring their sovereignty. Hyndland, where we moved, was a residential area with big houses and few shops. Our house was stone, semi-detached. We had the upstairs part. Downstairs lived an old couple who stared at us from the window in horror. The gravel driveway curved in a half circle, allowing my father to park his new blue Renault in front of the stone steps leading to the entrance. The licence plate read 339FFS ("three-three-nine fucking fucking shit," Ava cursed, threatening to scratch the side of the car with a nail file). Behind the glass-paneled door at the top of the stairs lay a long, dark hallway and five bedrooms, a living room, and a kitchen. Of the three bathrooms, one came with the master bedroom and was reserved for my parents; one had only a toilet in it, so the remaining one with a bath was to be shared by the kids. Each of us was allotted a bath once a week to stop us fighting over it.

At supper, in the pine booth in the kitchen, Kirk held up his fork. "Hey, this says Dougalls on it."

"So does mine," said Fig.

My mother shrugged. "We couldn't move into a house with nothing, could we," she said with a grimace.

Our street was so windy that when it rained—nearly every day—the rain pelted down sideways. New York had been covered in a blanket of heat, but in Scotland, there was no summer, no hot days and warm, balmy nights. Instead, it was freezing, and no matter how many heaters we used, a veneer of icy damp clung to everything, including our clothes. My bed, up against a stone wall, felt like the inside of a refrigerator.

Ava and Natalie shared a room across the hall from mine, and I spent most of the time in theirs, smoking cigarettes out the window when my parents went out looking for a movie. I lit a stack of tissues, surprised when the flame quickly shot to my fingers. Yowling, I threw the flaking pyre on the floor. Unfortunately, we were all barefoot.

"Oh my god!" gasped Natalie. She ran to the wardrobe for a boot to furiously stomp out the fire.

"You could have burned down the house," said Ava. For days, her face had been stamped with the same angry expression.

Natalie laughed bitterly. "That wouldn't have been such a bad idea. Maybe he'd let us go back."

"I am going back," said Ava. "I'm getting a job. I'm not staying in this place. He can go fuck himself."

I overheard her telling my father that later on.

"You are not getting a job!" he shouted. "You're staying at school until I say so."

"That's what you think," retorted Ava. "I'm sixteen. I don't have to go to school anymore. I'm getting a job."

"A job? What do you know about a job?"

Ava laughed angrily. "That's it. I want to find out."

For once, my father couldn't think of anything to say, and Ava started looking the next day. She went to the Employment

Office and got a job, typing for a company that made rubber parts for engines. But she didn't care what it was. All she wanted was to save money to return to New York. Just as she had with my mother's jewelry, she hid her pay underneath her mattress, probably reveling in it at night when she thought everyone was asleep. But this time, the cache belonged to her and she was going to use it to buy her freedom.

I thought all we had brought to Scotland were clothes, but the pin-scarred family portrait appeared in the living room, along with the two family photograph albums that had been in New York. My mother looked puffy inside her woolen skirts and sweaters as she hung the portrait on the flock wallpaper.

"I swear, this rain is going to drive me crazy," she said, getting off the stepstool to fish inside her pocket for a couple of painkillers. "Day in, day out. No wonder my sinuses are inflamed."

"Yeah, Mom," I said, trying to smile reassuringly.

Soon after, she refused to get up, due to illness, or so my father said after he had dropped her off at a hospital to recuperate. We visited her one night and traveled down unlit roads for miles before we reached her bedside. Looking wan in a hospital gown, she said hello in a weak voice. We left after a few minutes. Two weeks later, I found blood in my underpants. I ran to Natalie, frightened.

"It's your period," she said. She lent me a sanitary belt, and squeezing next to me in the small bathroom, showed me how to hook a pad onto it.

When my mother got home a few days later, I told her I'd got my period.

"Congratulations," she said in a strangely cheery voice. "You're a woman now." But her eyes were blank.

On a Sunday soon after we had started school, I ambled along with Ava and Natalie to scour Sauchiehall Street in the ghost of a downtown, with only the sound of sloshing tires of the few cars on the road to accompany us. Inside the store windows, drab, colorless sweaters and polyester dresses hung loosely on pale mannequins, looking gray and ghoulish through the pelting rain.

We sauntered through the streets with daisies picked from the roadside sprouting from our hair, hooting with laughter as a woman, huddled under a duffel coat and clutching a string bag to her chest, gaped at us from a bus stop. Then, our skin running with sweat and rain, we crashed into Dino's Café on Byers Road, Ava's scornful tone competing with the screeching of her chair as she kept getting up for another Coke. In between cigarettes, I squirted mustard and brown sauce into a sugar bowl. The owner, a mild enough man, threatened to kick us out for soiling his tables.

"Look at that creep," snorted Ava. Her thin bracelets jangled as she gestured with her thumb at a skinny man in a dull brown anorak ogling her over his cup of tea. His mouth hung open, showing crooked teeth. She tossed her head, making her hair bounce on her shoulders.

"Yeah, what a creep," I said loudly through her cloud of smoke.

She laughed mockingly. "It must be his lucky day, getting to sit near us." She flicked ash onto the plastic table and circled it with her finger.

"Yeah," I agreed.

Ava snorted again, pressing her white fingers into the tabletop. "What a prick. He's just looking for a parking spot."

"Ha-ha," I croaked, confused.

Natalie tilted her head as she lit another cigarette. "She doesn't know what you're talking about. She's too young."

"I am not," I said hotly.

Ava grinned maliciously. "Tell me then." She raised her eyebrows, waiting.

I put my head down, feeling a blush charge up my neck.

"Oh, forget it," said Ava after a pause, losing interest. "What the fuck does it matter anyway."

Ava soon stopped coming out with us. She worked all day and stayed out late. She seemed to forget all about us, but not Marcel, her boyfriend in New York, even after she had started dating David, a man whom my father met while buying furniture and set up with Ava, probably to keep an eye on her. Somehow she had received a bag of pot wrapped in a sock from Marcel. Hiding behind the house, she smoked it reefer by reefer, her eyes growing bloodshot and her speech slowing down until she sounded like a record on 16 speed. Clearly in her book, by that time it was each "geh-errrl" for herself.

I n Scotland, school was either Protestant or Catholic, just like gangs and football teams. My parents sized up the situation quickly and decided we were Protestant. No obligation to confess must have made it an easy choice.

I began my sixth school in four years. The headmaster didn't believe my mother when she said I belonged in a class a year above my age because I had skipped a year somewhere along the way.

"Och, no, we don't do that here," she was told, as if she had suggested overthrowing the government. So I was placed in the last year of elementary school—called a primary school—where I soon caused a disruption by asking for a pencil in a loud voice.

"No talking," scolded my teacher.

"Okay," I said agreeably.

Her face turned red. She sent me to the headmaster, Mr. Mutch, who sat me down in a chair across from his desk. He adjusted his glasses and looked down at me as if he were sucking a sour apple.

"In this country, we call our teachers Sir if they're men and Miss if they're not. You understand? So when your teacher asks you a question, you have to address her like this: 'Yes, Miss.' Not her name, just 'Miss.'"

His condescending tone made the hairs rise on the back of my neck. "Okay," I answered blandly, getting up to go.

"Sit down!" he said. "I did not give you permission to leave." His face bulged with rage. "And call me Sir!"

I cocked my head. "Okay."

Mr. Mutch looked like he was going to explode as he reached for a leather strap with a fringed tail hanging behind his desk. "You'll learn not to be insolent! You're in Scotland now, not America." He spat out America as if it were poison.

Grabbing my hands, he turned the palms upward and raised the strap above his head. He pelted me six times, staring at me fiercely all the while. I started crying after the second thwack. When it was over, he replaced the strap onto its hook and ordered me back to class.

My mother looked up from her magazine when I told her. "I guess that's how they do things here," she said. She tsked. "Try to stay out of trouble."

School imposed a whole bevy of new rules, beginning with language. I was not to say *Scotch* but *Scottish* when referring to people (a prickly subject), *ken* not *know*, *hen* not *sweetheart*, *stones* not *pounds*, *fortnight* not *two weeks*, and *shillings* and *pence*, not *dollars* and *cents*. Sometimes a whole string of words had to be translated in whole like *I dunny ken, hen, bu'*, meaning *I haven't a clue, sweetheart*. In the playground, I learned to say *shite* not *shit*, *arse* not *ass*, *aye* rather than *yes*, *ta* not *thanks*, *och* not *oh*, *the noo* instead of *now* or to emphasize *aye*, and *bogs* for *bathroom*. When I cried, I was laughed at for being a *wain* not a *child*. In history class, I learned that the country used to be ruled by *lairds* not *lords* who had lots of *bairns* not *babies*. Breakfast was still breakfast, but *lunch* was *dinner* and *supper* was *tea*. *High tea* was a more formal, food-laden tea and *supper* was a snack before bedtime. It was a wonder that people weren't too fat to leave their houses, all the eating they did.

Outside class, I learned to smoke for real, inhaling tiny Players No. 6s on the school roof. The first time I tried, I boasted so much that I knew how to inhale that I almost choked to death on the stairs leading up to the roof. But it did the trick and I was accepted into a gang of two.

Erica, red haired and freckled, had approached me in the school yard my second day of school. "Say 'Hi, honey,'" she said, chin jutting forward.

"Why?" I asked.

"I said, say 'Hi, honey.'"

"Aye," said Bridget.

"What?"

Erica pushed me. "Say it or . . ." A scrambled stream of words flowed out of her mouth.

I assessed the situation—two girls bigger than me, who belonged in this country.

"Hi, honey," I mumbled, feeling like an idiot.

"No." Erica shoved me. "Say it like they say it in the pictures."

My guess that pictures meant the movies was right. I put

a hand on my hip and said mockingly, "Hi, honey," in a loud nasally voice. The girls rolled around laughing.

"She's all right," said Bridget, slipping her arm around my shoulder. "Come to the bogs."

My new friends taught me how to moisten torn-off wads of tracing paper that served as toilet paper, each sheet inscribed with *HM Government Property.* The wads had just enough water to stick on the ceiling after we hurled them up there, so that they would drop on teachers when they came looking for us. After I left the school, I found out that the girls were locked up in a juvenile detention center for burning a classmate's legs with the ends of cigarettes. I had no trouble with them, just as long as I kept saying 'hi, honey.' They called me Beaky, mocking how my nose filled up my face.

Food and school blended together in domestic science, a class that sounded like something with test tubes until I discovered I now had to learn how to bake cakes and make Welsh rarebit. I thought the teacher said rabbit and turned up my nose, saying, "Ugh, I can't eat that," until I saw it was cheese sauce poured over toast. I also was to master the art of sculpting a repulsive mixture of sausage, batter, and egg that the teacher proudly called a Scotch egg. I learned a full range of Scottish fare at school and found it was very different from the steaks, pasta, and fresh vegetables we ate at home. Salad was no longer a bowl full of greens and sliced tomatoes, cucumber, carrots, and scallions in a dressing of oil and vinegar. It was a thin slice of cucumber and one-half of a small, sad-looking tomato balanced precariously on a single leaf of lettuce and a glob of yellow-white sauce called salad cream. There was vinegar in everything—and sugar. All food was floured and fried and butchered beyond recognition. And then there were chips. Egg and chips, chicken and chips, beefburger and chips, fish and chips—I even learned how to make a sandwich with them, placing a handful between two thin slices of margarined bread. Black pudding was the one thing I adamantly refused to eat, in spite of Miss lecturing me on its merits. The congealed blood sausage of a purplish-red hue turned my stomach, and when I had to prepare it, I stuck little balls of tissue up my nose to hide the smell.

The more strict and disapproving the teachers, the more I fought back. My French teacher proudly announced to the class that Scottish people had the best French accents because of the way they rolled the letter *r*. What about me, I thought, too inexperienced to know that in any case it wasn't true because the Scottish *r* is at the front of the mouth and the French at the back. But it gave me a good slogan—Rrrroll your arrrrrse—which I practiced in class, much to the annoyance of Mademoiselle. My knitting teacher was allergic to peppermints. Erica and I sucked on them so we could watch her increasing agitation while she circled the classroom with runny nose and eyes. I didn't even like peppermints, but the burn on my tongue was worth it.

At home, my mother had recovered her old equanimity by what should have been spring, except it was still raining and cold. She yelled at me for not peeling the potatoes and slapped me when I talked back. I remembered the fuck-off girls in New York and hit her back—not hard, just a tap, but all the same to let her know I wasn't going to stand for it anymore.

"How dare you!" she screamed in horror, but she never hit me again.

After I'd been at school for a few months and had made several trips to the headmaster, I started a competition over who could jump the most stairs at once. I landed on my ankle and had to stay home for three weeks while the sprain mended. The headmaster called my mother and said I was too advanced and should start at Hyndland Secondary where Natalie and Kirk were already in attendance. The Protestant school was public but called state just like the primary school, whereas private schools were called public, making my head turn even more. I was not to be put into Kirk's class as it wasn't healthy, the headmaster said. "And by the way," Mr. Mutch noted, "that girl needs an eye on her—a right nuisance she is."

"Maybe you won't be hit at the new school," said my mother when she told me the news.

With my sprained foot in a bandage, I read magazines with my mother on the patch of grass at the front of the house on rare days that the sun peeked out of the clouds. Now that she was spending most days alone, with us at school, Marilyn at nursery school, and Ava at work, she liked the company that illness brought. She sat with four-ply toilet paper wrapped around her head so that her hair wouldn't be spoiled and swallowed painkillers for her sinuses.

"Can I have one, too?" I asked.

She gave me half a dose and smiled, saying, "Here's a magazine. I just finished it."

So, while sitting next to her in a matching lawn chair, I read about the royal family and how to apply eye shadow so men would think I was sophisticated but not threatening, just like my mother.

When my ankle was better, I started at Hyndland. The long rows of windows on every floor were the only things open about it. We were not permitted to speak unless called on by the teacher, who never called on anyone who raised her hand, least of all me, the only foreigner in the class. In my history class, I learned that Britain was Great and had brought civilization to savages all over the world.

"Yes, Tosca, your people, too."

"We're not savages," I protested.

Miss ignored me and went back to the map covered in red to denote which countries Britain had conquered, O Britannia. I was taught that the best inventors in the world were Scottish and the best thinkers English. Welsh people had good voices and the Irish built everything. The finest dances were Scottish jigs—which I was forced to learn in gym class—and the heartiest food potatoes. I also learned that in Britain, Great though it was, there was a royal family that ruled only in name and that a government—"much like hers," said the teacher, pointing at me—made all the decisions.

"But why, Miss? Why is there a queen if she doesn't do anything?" I asked, confused.

"To preserve our democracy."

"But it doesn't make sense. Why don't you just get a president?"

Miss raised her eyebrows. "Maybe it would be better if you had a queen."

"Why? What difference would it make?"

She sighed loudly. "Tosca Rung, why do you have to be so obstreperous? Class, turn to page three and we'll continue."

I turned to my new friend, Cathie Stewart. "Queen Bitch," I mouthed.

Cathie burst out laughing and was sent to the headmaster for the strap. She was Catholic but ended up in my school because her father was drunk when he signed the papers. She lived in the Gorbals, the poorest area of the city. Tall and dark with long, stringy hair that she wore in a ponytail at the nape of her neck, Cathie became my best friend because she was as miserable as me. She lived in a two-room flat in a crumbling tenement building. There was only one toilet in the whole building, and it sat in a dark, cold stairwell. Instead of toilet paper, a stack of torn-off pieces of newspaper lay on the floor, some of which were still greasy from holding take-out chips.

In front of me, Cathie's father slapped her mother for serving his dinner cold. Cathie pressed against the wall, crying soundlessly while her mother closed her eyes and picked up his plate. I hoped she was going to throw it at him, but she only shuffled to the oven and put it back in. Cathie was determined to be different from them. She wanted to go technical college or, if she could get a grant, university. But our teacher set her straight, telling her that she'd be better off getting a job.

"But I want to go to college," Cathie insisted, a crease lining her forehead.

"Be realistic," said Miss tightly.

Cathie had glared at her and stormed out of the room. I followed her into the bogs.

"What does she mean?" I asked.

Cathie's eyes filled with tears. "They're all the fucking same. I thought she was different. They think just because I'm working class I can't go to college. It's only for rich people." She spat out the words, and I felt guilty because my father had money and hers didn't.

"Don't worry, Cathie. My sister got a job even though my father said she couldn't."

She shrugged me off and lit a cigarette. Looking hard at the floor, she said bitterly, "I'm going to run away if he hits me again."

"Yeah, you should," I agreed emphatically. I didn't realize that my father beat me, too. My mother said only poor parents hit their children. We were rich, at least compared to Cathie, so that meant my father didn't do what hers did.

Cathie became more and more angry and spent all her time smoking cigarettes in the toilets. I joined in her rebellion, though I stopped short of wearing my skirt at the top of my thighs as the risk of humiliation from fat knees was greater than the fun of inciting the teachers' fury. Our uniform was red and black, the colors of anarchy, something that must have worried the teachers for they kept such tight wraps on our behavior.

"Three inches below the knees, girls," scolded the headmistress at assembly.

When our religious education teacher thought we were all safely absorbed in his class assignments, he dropped pencils on the floor so he could bend down and look up our skirts. He had a routine all worked out. First he would scratch his head, then his beard, then quickly pick his nose and rummage behind his ear. It was after the ear motion that he would drop a pencil. Cathie watched him under one drooped eyelid, and at the appropriate moment, stretched her legs wide so she could watch him squirm. One day, she placed a soiled tampon between her legs and Sir turned so red, I thought he was going to have a heart attack. He stopped dropping things for a while after that. By the time he started up again, Cathie had been suspended for swearing at a teacher.

"I don't give a shite," she said, tossing her hair.

Every Sunday, my father ordered us to shush while he listened to the dry voice of Alistair Cooke's *Letter from America* on the radio. "Today, President Johnson is facing one of the most important decisions of his presidency."

I wondered if my father missed being at home, as I did.

"Ah, New York," he said as if to dismiss the thought. "Dirty, violent. It's lucky we left." Lucky for who, I thought. But I didn't dare say anything. My parents had said we had come here for Ava's good while she continued to stuff money under her mattress, and also because the Vietnam War was escalating and would take my brothers. So, whenever anyone asked why we had moved to Scotland, that's what I said. I didn't know how to respond when they asked what my father did. I approached my mother for the answer.

"Tell them it's none of their business," she said, pursing her lips to apply another coat of orange. She had just shaved her eyebrows and penciled in new ones so that she looked permanently surprised.

"But, Mom, I can't," I pleaded. "They'll make fun of me."

She waved her hand. "Then just tell them he's an economist."

"What's that?"

"For god's sake, make something up. You're a smart girl. You'll think of something."

ran into Erica at Dino's before the manager kicked me out for messing up his sugar bowls again. She'd just been let out of detention and moved into an old-age home owned by her father and run by a housekeeper. Her mother was dead or gone, I couldn't remember which and didn't want to be rude in case she beat me up. Her lips were buttoned about what it had been like in detention, or what had happened to the girl whose legs she'd burned.

"What school do you go to now?" I asked, remembering how she'd terrorized me into saying 'hi, honey' at primary school.

"Kelvinside Secondary. We moved. My dad opened up an old-age home." Her eyes kept shifting to the side as she talked, her brows locked together into a frown.

I looked at her in surprise. She seemed so cowed, miserable, nothing like the little toughie I'd known at school.

"If you're not doing anything, why don't you come over for dinner?" she asked with her eyes averted, her face pale and freckly.

I shrugged. "Okay."

The old-age home rose tall and rectangular behind shrubs of exploding pale pink rhododendron, with rows of tightly sashed windows surrounded by rain-stained stone on the outside and glossy yellow wallpaper on the inside. On the housekeeper's face lay a bed of wrinkles, and she wore a white linen coat and cap while she served us tea. Erica glared at her with hostility, then put her face down to eat from the thin china plate ringed with tiny pink roses. She wouldn't look up to catch my eye. Hurt, I wondered why she'd asked me to come.

I observed carefully how Erica picked up the fork with her

left hand and the knife with her right, and I copied her so the housekeeper wouldn't turn her beady eyes on me. Dinner was a fried egg, bacon, sausage, baked beans, and chips with a grilled tomato. I wasn't used to eating with a knife, and when I pressed it into the egg, the knife slid against the bacon, which pushed against the tomato. I tried to grab the tomato, but I couldn't stop its flight. I shrieked as it slammed into the scoured wall, then stared at it, horrified. The tomato had smashed right under a picture of idling cows in a pasture and dripped down the wall in a stream of grease.

"Sorry," I choked, then burst into giggles as I tried to wipe it off the wall.

"What?" asked Erica, looking up for an instant. "Never mind," she said, and went back to her food.

I clenched my jaws to stop giggling and rearranged my features so I would have a serious expression on my face. But I couldn't stop laughing, and strange honking noises escaped from my nose. I put my head down, pretending not to notice as I kept on honking.

"Ner-r-r-vous, isn't she," the housekeeper said as she poured herself another cup of thick black tea from the pot set at the middle of the table.

"Aye," said Erica sullenly. She scraped back her chair and got up, barely glancing at me. "I've got to do my homework."

I followed her out stiffly, still shaking with laughter.

"She's a fucking weirdo," I muttered to myself as I walked home in the pouring rain.

But Erica was the only person I knew with a telephone so I called her one Sunday to ask what she was doing.

"Nothing," she said. "Fancy going to Loch Lomond?"

"What is it?"

She sounded incredulous. "You don't know Loch Lomond? Everybody knows it!"

"Of course I do!" I cleared my throat. "I was just testing you." I was glad she didn't see my discomfort. I didn't dare tell her I'd never heard of Scotland either, not before we'd moved. The nearest place I'd heard about was Liverpool because that was where the Beatles were from, and that was two hundred miles away in another country. "I'll come over to your house."

"No, I'll meet you at the underground."

I ran to the station and skipped down a stone staircase to the one platform where a half-empty train waited—wooden and red and rickety, like a toy. After I pulled open the doors and went inside, I sat on one of the bare seats and looked around. A middle-aged woman with red legs and three string bags crammed full of onions, carrots, leeks, and potatoes yanked a brown-haired boy onto the seat beside her. I smiled at her, but she ignored me and rummaged in her bags for a bright green apple she gave to the boy.

When the train creaked to a halt, I found Erica on the platform twisting a limp strand of hair. "Got any fags?" she asked.

"No, do you?"

"Bloody hell, no. Hey mister, got any fags?" she asked the ticket collector.

"Och, lassie, you shouldn't be smoking."

"Aye, but I do."

The man pulled on his handlebar mustache. "What will your mother say if she knows I've been corrupting you?"

"She's dead so you don't have to worry."

The man's eyes grew cloudy, and he reached over to pat her head. "Poor lassie, here you go." And he gave her a Woodbine, not even noticing me at her side.

Outside the station, a woman dressed in rags called out "Prostitutes!" for our smoking in the street.

"Not yet!" Erica shouted, making us laugh raucously as we skipped away.

Loch Lomond was northwest of the city, and we had to take British Rail to get there. On the train, Erica told me that her housekeeper had disappeared in the middle of the night and that later her father had found out that she had been stealing food from the pantry and selling it on the side.

"Is your father a thief?" she asked.

I jerked away from the midge-spattered window. "What?" I asked.

"Why else doesn't he tell anybody what he does?"

"How dare you call my father a thief? Take it back!"

Erica crossed her arms. "Well? Why else don't you know what he does?"

"I don't know! I think he's working for someone called Mr. McKenzie. Anyway, it's none of your business."

"Och, don't get your knickers in a twist. I didn't mean anything." She viewed me quizzically. "Why have you got a daisy in your hair?"

"*Everyone* does it," I said condescendingly.

After the train stopped, we walked to the edge of town. Everywhere was green, splashed with tiny purple flowers that I picked up and added to the collection on my head. I took off my shoes.

"Come on, walk barefoot with me."

"You must be mad," she said. "You're lucky I'm walking with you at all."

"Very funny."

We came to a lake, deep and blue and so wide I couldn't see the other side. Suddenly, I realized Loch Lomond was a lake. I dipped my feet into the icy water and watched as a school of tiny fishes slivered by.

"Hey, Erica," I said. "Will you still come and visit me when I go back to America?"

"Of course. Why?"

"I don't know." I looked down. The water had cleared, leaving no sign of the fish. I sucked my finger and scowled. "I want to go back."

"Why? Scotland's bonny. Everyone says so."

"America's better," I retorted defiantly.

"That's not true. My father says Americans are greedy pigs and want to buy up the whole world."

"At least they don't stare at you if you come from somewhere else!" I said hotly.

"Well, you should be lucky you didn't go to England. Bloody Sassanacks, talking out of their arses."

I giggled as I swung my legs under the water. "My mother likes England," I said, then added casually, "My parents went there on their way back to America from Russia."

Erica looked surprised. "Russia?"

"They didn't really go," I stuttered. "I mean, they sort of thought about going but—"

She looked at me strangely as I abruptly changed the subject. "What's your new school like?"

Cathie arrived back at Hyndland scowling at Miss with her eyes averted during roll call. We sneaked into the bogs during break and smoked one cigarette after another until the last bell rang. Then we tried to flush our schoolwork down the toilet and ran barefoot down Hyndland Road, swinging our school bags and laughing hysterically at anyone who passed us. I tripped on the curb and fell on a piece of glass, cutting my big toe. By the time I got back to my house, my toe had swollen up into a purple throbbing ball.

"For god's sake, wasn't hurting your ankle good enough?" said my mother, instructing my father to take me to the hospital after supper. We drove silently all the way there. I didn't dare make a sound as he seemed so preoccupied. Halfway up the driveway stood a sign: Dead Slow.

"I guess no one comes out of here alive." My father chuckled.

I let out a fake laugh. Wheelchairs lay in a row at the front door, but I followed my father on foot to the emergency waiting room, my toe throbbing.

Across from where we sat down in the waiting room, a boy with auburn hair faced us with what looked like a hole in his knee, leaking pus. His mother sat next to him, dressed in a floral housecoat. She reached over to brush hair out of her boy's eyes.

"Stop it, Mum," he said, twisting away. "I'm all right."

Makeshift screens fenced us in, behind which a woman talked in a low voice. Only the four of us were there, waiting in silence beneath fluorescent lights that drained the room of color.

"We've been here two hours," said the boy's mother in response to my father's question. "A nurse keeps coming out to look, then she's off again."

My father sucked the air between his teeth and lit a cigarette. "National Health," he muttered, sending a swirl of smoke in my direction.

I tried to think of something intelligent to say. He picked up a magazine and leafed through it, rustling the pages as if they were so many things to be discarded. His tapping foot betrayed his irritation at having to be there. From the corner of my eye,

I carried out an inspection. He had little bags under his eyes and black stubble protruding from his chin, but his suit was unrumpled and new. His skin was lined and soft and emitted a delicate fragrance of Old Spice and ashtrays. Time and again, his fingers reached for a cigarette that he lit with the butt of another. He didn't look like a thief. Thieves wore black leather and covered their faces with masks. I didn't know what Erica was talking about.

"Dad, nothing's going to happen to you, is it?" I asked nervously.

"What?" He looked up from his magazine with a frown. "Don't be ridiculous. What are you talking about?"

I sat back, appeased but at the same time bitten by his quick anger. My eye caught the boy's, and I shrugged. I counted the black hands of the clock. After sixteen minutes, a nurse came in and ushered out the boy and his mother. After twenty-two, my father stretched and yawned loudly, then stood on his feet.

"Can you do something for me, Tosca?"

"Yes," I said quickly.

"Can you be a big girl and wait here by yourself? I have some important things to take care of."

"Sure, Dad, I'll be okay." I nodded reassuringly.

He reached into his pocket and gave me threepence for the bus. "I'll see you at home." Placing an awkward hand on my head, he walked out the door and didn't look back.

As soon as he was gone, I felt a chill from the open window, blowing in the night air. Making circles in my thumb with a forefinger in boredom, I waited for my name to be called. Finally, a nurse came out and set me onto a flat table in the treatment room beneath a naked lightbulb.

"Lie there and wait for the doctor," she said, hands on hips. "Where's your father?"

"He left. He had something important to do."

Her eyes creased. "I don't know about that," she said. "What could be more important than a wounded child?" She stepped back. "My, what sad eyes you've got. Where's your mother?"

"She's at home," I answered noncommittally.

The nurse shook her head. "You're awfully young to be out on your own this late."

A doctor breezed into the room. "Nurse, please go up to Ward C to give Dr. Bodey's notes to the sister."

"Good-bye, dear," said the nurse. "Look after yourself." She left the room still shaking her head.

The doctor briskly examined my toe. "You'll just need a few stitches. No one will know the difference." He reached onto his tray for some gauze. "It's a good thing it's not your nose!" He smiled down at me. "Look at the wall and count to one hundred. I'll be through in no time."

I gritted my teeth and did what he said with tears of pain sliding into my ears. He didn't seem to realize that the overhead light threw shadows on the wall and magnified his movements. The giant hand went round and round on the eerie pale green wall as he swabbed my toe clean and stitched it up. When he was done, I let myself off the table and hobbled across the street to take the bus.

I was the only person on the dark street as I waited at the bus stop beneath a dim streetlight. A man in a white sports car stopped nearby, then backed up with a loud rumble until he was right next to me.

"Want a lift?" he asked, smiling across at me. Wavy blond hair framed his cheery face, and a thin beard grazed his chin.

I shook my head, trying to look angry so he would go away.

"Come on, hen. You'll have to wait ages for a bus."

"No, thanks," I said stiffly.

He leaned across the front seat, sticking his elbow on the window ledge of the passenger seat. "Are you sure? I won't bite you."

I squinted at him. "Do you have a light?" I said cockily. I pulled out a cigarette stub I'd been saving.

He laughed, his teeth small and square. "Aye, here you are."

I leaned closer, breathing in when his flame flickered at the tip of my cigarette. I jumped back before he could pull me into the car. "Thanks."

"Are you sure you don't want a lift?" he said.

"Yes," I answered forcefully.

The man seemed bemused and rode off with a loud honk.

I puffed on my cigarette feeling proud of myself and like I was pretty. The bus finally came, way after I'd smoked the cigarette halfway down the filter.

After the bus let me off on Hyndland Road, I limped down the street to our corner where a small block of flats with a bumpy concrete surface loomed. A man walked a large dog on the small patch of grass outside, standing by while his dog lifted its leg and peed against a rubbish bin. The dog looked up as I hobbled by, staring at me with dark, glistening eyes. I stared back. Without warning, he leaped up and jumped on me, knocking me down. With a thud, I slammed onto the pavement with him on top of me. I screamed and pushed him as hard as I could, his hot belly suffocatingly heavy on my chest.

"Charlie, heel!" The man whistled and the dog stopped, then stood back, growling.

"You should watch your fucking dog," I panted, pulling myself up.

"There's no need to swear," said the man in a mild voice. "You should never stare at dogs, especially German shepherds. Don't you know that?"

"Fuck off," I said, and continued limping to my house.

When I arrived home, only the hall light was on, spilling dimly onto the gravel. I staggered up the stairs, resting my arms on the banister, wobbling from exhaustion. My father's voice wafted through my parents' bedroom door as he told my mother to remember to pick up his suit from the cleaners. My mother appeared at the sound of the front door closing.

"Oh, it's you," she said. "Go to bed, school tomorrow."

On Valentine's Day, a card lay on my chair at school. "Dear Valentine," it read. "Meet me on Saturday outside Dino's at seven and I'm yours."

"Cathie," I whispered. "Who wrote this?"

Cathie glanced over my shoulder. "I dunny ken."

I scrutinized the faces of the boys in my class. I was happy all week. No boy had ever fancied me before.

A few months earlier, my father had sat me down for a talk. After loosening his tie, he'd said, "Every day I read about eleven-year-old girls getting pregnant, and I don't want to read about you."

First I'd thought to correct him, to tell him I was twelve. I looked at him, puzzled, not sure why he was reprimanding me. I had barely even kissed a boy, and that was way back in New York when I graduated elementary school.

He flicked ash. "If I ever catch you, believe you me, you'll be sorry *you* were born."

I understood that going out with boys meant getting pregnant, but I knew it wasn't true because Natalie had a boyfriend and she wasn't pregnant. So when I decided to find out who my Valentine was, I did what she did and told a lie. "I'm going to see a movie with some girls from school," I said.

"May I," corrected my mother, absently wiping the surface of the counter. "Aaron, what do you think? Can she go out tonight?"

My father's face emerged over his paper. "Why, has she been a good girl lately?"

My mother took up the tease. Both their faces were flushed. "Well, I wouldn't exactly say good but fair, yes, she's been fair. Tosca hasn't been in trouble for at least a week."

I drew my hair over my face, trying not to sulk.

"Well, okay," said my father, "but you have to home by nine."

Slipping out at at six-thirty in case my parents changed their minds, I stood on the corner of Byers Road, counting the minutes until it was exactly five past seven. Then I went to stand outside the café. That was what Natalie had told me to do, to be five minutes late. "Then he won't think you're too eager," she explained.

Casually, I turned my head one way and then the other, not wanting to be caught looking anxious. The street was empty, and I shivered as a breeze picked up and swept twigs along the street. A large Closed sign hung on Dino's door. I squinted inside the window. The clock had the same time as my watch: seven-twenty. I lit a cigarette and blew smoke rings, trying to pace it so that by the time the cigarette was gone, whoever had written the note would be there. I lit another cigarette. Seven-thirty. Another. Seven-fifty.

At eight-ten, I realized there was no point in waiting any longer. Probably a joke, I thought bitterly, crushing the butt against the wall. Just someone trying to make me look like a fool. I turned the corner, glad that at least no one had seen me.

I walked the empty streets, hands in my pockets, feeling ugly. But I wasn't going to get into trouble over it and lingered so I wouldn't return home before nine in case my father became suspicious.

At a few minutes past nine, I crept down the hallway to my room, shivering with disappointment and cold. I silently clicked the door closed behind me and switched on the light. My father's voice made me jolt. He was rocking slowly on my rocking chair near the window.

"You're late," he said, pointing to his watch.

"I'm sorry, Dad. The movie just got out," I lied swiftly.

"Oh, yes? What movie did you see?"

"*Psycho*," I stuttered. I'd overheard some girls talking about it in the changing room at school.

"What's it about?"

I stumbled over my words, hoping he would leave me alone to cry into my pillow. "There's this woman in the shower and a man stabs her. And there's all this blood. It was really scary and . . ." My throat dried up as I noticed my father's fingers impatiently tap the side of the chair.

"What time did it start?"

"Seven o'clock," I said smoothly.

"What time did it finish?"

"Eight-thirty."

"So it took you thirty-five minutes to walk home. I presume you did walk home?"

"Of course." The blue cord disappeared from his neck. Relieved, I let out my breath.

"Spell it."

"C-y-c-o," I said confidently.

His hand moved so fast, I didn't see it coming. His sour breath was hot on my face as he pinned me to the wall.

"Who do you think you're dealing with?" he screamed. "What do you take me for, an idiot?"

"No, Dad, no!" I shrieked, twisting my head to the side.

"Didn't I warn you not to lie to me? Didn't I?" His hair swung crazily over his brow.

My mother poked her head around the door. "What's going on in here?" she asked, frowning.

"Mom! Tell him to stop hitting me!"

"Shh, you'll wake everyone up. Keep it down in here, will you?"

"Stop hitting me!" I tried to free myself from his grip. "You have no right to hit me!"

My father blinked a few times, then seemed to get me back in focus. He shook his head, growling that I should go to bed.

My mother stabbed her finger in the air between us. "You shouldn't upset him like this."

"You shouldn't upset him," I mimicked angrily, but not until they were out of the room and the door was tightly closed. I lay down, crying until all feeling was washed out of me. Then I charged up and shoved three pairs of underwear and a shirt into a bag.

The hallway was dark, no lines of light appearing from underneath anyone's door, except from my parents' room at the front. Stealthily, I eased myself out the front entrance. Then I turned toward Cathie's house on the other side of the city.

I sped all the way there, passing pubs filled with smoke and people singing drunkenly with their arms around each other. Near the train station, three men crouched over a barrel of flames, sharing a bottle of methylated spirits. Unnoticed, I slipped by in the shadows, blowing on my hands to warm them.

Cathie had been waiting with her mother at their kitchen table for her father to come home from the pub. "What are you doing here?" she asked, surprised to find me on her doorstep.

"My father hit me," I said simply.

Cathie nodded knowingly. "Come in."

Cathie's mother came out and observed my bag. Her face was shiny and drawn. "You cannae stay here. Cathie's father will go spare if he sees you."

"Why, Mum?" asked Cathie argumentatively. "She's done nothing wrong."

Her mother rubbed her eyes wearily. Cathie's lips tightened, and she reached for her coat. "I'm taking her to Aileen's, then."

Her sister lived a few blocks away in a tenement the same as Cathie's. Only the numbers painted in black above the entrance told them apart.

"Fucking bastards," said Cathie, edging down the dark stairway. "I'd like to murder them all."

When Aileen opened the door, the smell of old diapers

spilled into the unlit hallway. "All right, she can stay but just for tonight." She looked down at me with a worried expression. "I'm sorry, hen, my husband's still in the nick, and I can't take the risk of the police finding you here."

At my look of desperation, she shook her head. "I'm sorry, there's nothing I can do. My own father's the same way. You just have to wait until you're old enough to leave home."

"I'll never be old enough." My voice was wooden.

"Aye," said Aileen tiredly, picking up her baby and holding her to her breast. She handed Cathie a coin from a sugar canister perched behind a teapot on top of her kitchen cabinet. "Ring her father and tell him she'll be home in the morning."

Cathie squeezed my arm before she left. "I'll be back to go home with you. He won't dare lift a finger if I'm there." She turned to hug me, muttering, "I'll kill him if he does."

The sofa was frayed and lumpy. Hardly breathing, I lay still as a rock and watched car lights as they crept across the ceiling and were swallowed up by the gaping darkness. The only sounds were the baby coughing in the next room and a drunk kicking a can on the street. It was hopeless. I would have to wait, just like Cathie, until I was old enough to leave. At least now, with Cathie taking me home, I'd be safe. He would never hit me in front of anyone.

As promised, Cathie came with me in the morning. The farther we walked from her house, the lower and fatter the buildings became, eventually turning into large, multi-bedroomed houses with front lawns and bay windows. Cathie became increasingly silent, shoving her hands in her pockets and tossing her head as if she were angry.

As we crept up my driveway my father's face appeared in the upstairs window. "Don't leave me," I pleaded.

Cathie scowled. "Of course I won't." But her eyes were distant, half-closed.

My father threw open the front door, hair was slicked down and face freshly shaved. "Well, hello there, stranger," he said, grinning widely as if he were happy to see me. "And whom do I have the pleasure of meeting?" He smiled warmly at Cathie. "You must be Cathie. Tosca has told us so much about you."

I gulped. I'd barely mentioned her. My father led us upstairs and offered Cathie a glass of milk. "So nice to have one of Tosca's friends here. She's so secretive, you know. She never likes to bring anyone home."

"That's not true!" I protested.

But Cathie was deaf to me as she gaped at the flock wallpaper dotted with framed pictures and a long hallway carpeted in lush green. A bitter lump formed in my throat as she said in wonder, "I didn't know your house was so big."

"Would you like a tour?" my father offered graciously, dipping a hand solicitously in hers. "Come, I'll show you." As he guided her from room to room, he pointed out books and ornaments my mother had bought in the most expensive stores in town. With my hope that Cathie could save me drowning in the pool of my father's deceit, I hardly noticed when the tour was over and Cathie said in a funny voice, "I have to go now. My mother needs me."

"Thank you for bringing her home," my father said affably. "Come again, whenever you like." He held the door open, grasping my upper arm to keep me inside. "Don't believe everything Tosca says. You know how kids like to exaggerate."

Cathie squared her shoulders, proud he was taking her into his confidence, feeling mature, better, and more grown up than me, her best friend. "Aye, Mr. Rung, I know what you mean." Then, without as much as a cursory glance, she disappeared down the stairs and down the driveway.

My father's smile vanished as soon as she was gone. He gripped my arm tighter. Red poured into his face. His eyes pierced through me. "How dare you go to someone's house and tell lies like that. If you bring her here again, I'll kill you!"

Cathie wouldn't catch my eye after that and avoided me at school. When I bumped into her sister in the market, Aileen lowered her head and said, "Cathie thinks you're an awful liar. She thinks you made it up just so you could look big." She picked up her groceries and loaded them into the back of the baby carriage. "She said your dad wouldn't hurt a fly."

"It's not true!" I blurted angrily. But she was already gone.

n Glasgow, instead of changing cities or countries, we changed rooms. First I had my own room, then Kirk and Fig were fighting too much, so Kirk got my room. Fig went off to share with Rock, and I moved into Kirk's old room and shared with Marilyn. Then Ava got the single room, Kirk and Fig shared again, and Rock and Marilyn got together, the only time my parents let a boy and a girl sleep in the same room. Natalie and I shared a room for a while, but then she and Ava hatched a plan to share again because all of a sudden they were best friends, just like in New York. So now I moved again, this time into the single room at the back of the house. They were older than I so I had to. Only my parents stayed in one place, in the master bedroom with its own bathroom at the end of the hall near the front door.

Even while my father listened to Alistair Cooke on the radio for news of home, he wore a cagey expression, like he was being hunted. He cocked his ear as if listening to a voice no one else could hear. Every so often he shifted his shoulders as if shrugging something off and then would jump up to do something, like close the door. He kept the doors shut as if they were chapters of his life he had closed for good. He acted as if he couldn't remember anything, like the past was only good for one thing, forgetting.

Kirk had been off school with the flu. My mother told him she was angry that my father never took her on his business trips. When my father returned, Kirk asked innocently, "Dad, why don't you ever take Mom anywhere?"

"How dare you question my authority," yelled my father.

"But Dad, I was only asking."

My brother ducked as my father's fist flew through the air,

and he made a run for it. My father chased him outside as Kirk sped into the rain dressed only in blue pajamas.

"You're not going to hit me!" Kirk screamed.

They spun around the garden, still wet from an early morning downpour, until Kirk skidded and fell down. In a split second, he was up again and just escaped my father's grip by weaving in and around the neatly trimmed hedges.

Finally, my father caught him by the scruff of his neck. Twisting the collar of his pajama top with one hand, and stretching out his other for balance, my father kicked him back into the house. The other kids made themselves scarce, but I stood at the foot of the stairs, unable to move as my father kicked Kirk upstairs, bouncing him one step at a time while Kirk screamed at the top of his lungs. That Kirk had almost died two years earlier must have been one of my father's closed chapters, something else he couldn't remember.

CHAPTER EIGHT

MIRROR MIRROR

After we'd lived in Glasgow for over a year, my mother rounded us up in the olive-green living room for a family portrait.

"Put on something nice," she said as she applied another layer of orange lipstick to the area just above her lip line. "The photographer's coming at eleven."

"Aw, Mom," I complained. "Do we have to?"

Her idea of dress clothes was a thick woolen skirt in brown and beige plaid and skin-colored tights made for someone with skin two shades darker than mine.

"Yes, you do," she said. Bra straps showed through the opening in the back of her dress as she turned and poured a glass of water. One, two, down the pills went. She pressed her lips with the edge of a kitchen towel. "And tie your hair back."

"No," I cried.

"Tie your hair back I said!"

My mother yanked my hair into a ponytail, making it lie flat on my head. Everything stood out—my too big eyes, my too thin lips, my bumpy nose and short forehead. When she turned away, I pulled down a few strands for cover. As she went to change clothes, her hands buzzed around her own face, as if making sure that everything was still there.

At eleven o'clock, I hid in the bathroom smoking a cigarette, hoping no one would notice my absence. But the photographer, a burly man who kept on his raincoat, had been told there were seven children, and when he lined everybody up, he counted only six. Natalie was sent to look for me.

"Hurry up!" she called through the door. "Everyone's waiting."

"This is stupid!" I called out angrily.

She sighed. "It'll be over soon. Just smile like the fucker says."

I dragged on my cigarette and thought about escaping out the window, but it was too small, and besides, I was on the second story. So I stubbed out my cigarette, sprayed air freshener, flung my head back, and in case anyone still didn't get the message, stalked into the living room with my eyes on the ceiling, tsking loudly.

The whole family was lined up in front of the bay windows. On the window seat, my mother had placed large bouquets of plastic roses. She and my father stood at the back with Natalie and Ava on either side. Natalie clasped her hands behind her back so no one could see the eczema that had broken out. Head bowed, Ava glared at the floor in repressed rage. Rock and Marilyn kneeled at the front, and behind were Fig and Kirk.

"Get over here," snapped my mother as she stepped out of line and pushed me between my two brothers.

"I want to stand next to Natalie," I protested.

"Shut up," hissed my father dangerously close to my ear.

"Smile!" called the photographer brightly, angling his camera. A blinding flash caught me frowning.

"I'll have to take another one," he said, adjusting a lens but still cheery. "Keep still, everyone!"

"I don't want to have my picture taken," I cried, breaking out of formation. "This is stupid."

"Get back here!" My father pressed his fingers hard into my shoulder and steered me back in line.

"Say cheese!"

I burst into tears. "No one ever asked me if I wanted to have my picture taken."

"Oh for god's sake," said my mother. "What's wrong with her?"

The photographer blinked nervously and fidgeted with the knob of the camera as if that were causing the problem.

"Can't somebody do something with her?" My mother's question hung over us like a thundercloud.

Rock twisted around, his freckles standing out on his pale cheeks. "Can't you just smile for a minute? I have to go to the bathroom." He squirmed as if he were about to do it right there.

My father chuckled, then Kirk, and soon laughter was sweeping up and down the rows. I giggled nervously.

The photographer sprang into position and aimed his

camera. "Great shot!" he said as another flash exploded in the air.

"Take another one, now!" ordered my mother. "Before she starts crying again."

I burst into tears again. "You're all crazy! How can you stand here smiling when everything's so horrible? I hate it here! I hate Scotland! It's stupid pretending we're so happy!"

Ava's voice was sulky, low. "You're not the only one who feels like that, you know."

I turned around, furious. "So why doesn't anyone else say anything?"

She blinked a few times, then went back to glaring at the floor.

"You should know just how lucky you are," my father said coldly.

The photographer packed up the last of his equipment and turned to us. "What a lovely family. The pictures should come out splendidly." But his voice sounded an octave too high, like a mouse caught in a cupboard.

"Yes, yes," said my mother brightly, ushering him out.

Natalie was putting on an army shirt over jeans when I walked into the room she shared with Ava. Ava lay on her bed with a transistor radio under her pillow. A wooden wardrobe split the room in half, with a large mirror facing Natalie's side. As Natalie bent down in front of it to roll up her jeans, her wavy hair swung low over her face. I bent down and let my hair cover my face, too.

Shoving aside her school uniform on the bed, I sat down and said wistfully, "You're so pretty. I wish I could look like you."

Natalie glanced at me in surprise through her new glasses she'd suddenly had to start wearing. They were gold-rimmed and round, like John Lennon's. "But you are pretty."

"No, I'm not. Look at my nose, it's horrible. I wish it was straight like yours."

Natalie turned away, pulling out her shirt. Then, after a cursory look in the mirror, she tucked it in again. "Your nose is strong," she said. "It's powerful."

"If it's so powerful, why does everyone always make fun of me?" Just last week, a boy in the school yard had pointed as I walked by on my way to lunch. "Beaky, beaky, where's your birdseed?" I had spun around and spit at his feet, but that only made him laugh louder.

Natalie shrugged and adjusted her collar. "It's because you are so powerful. Maybe people are scared of you and they pretend they're not by making fun of you."

I frowned. "I thought people laughed at you because you're ugly."

My sister peered into the closet mirror. "Maybe you're right," she said. She rummaged through the bottom of the wardrobe and pulled out rainbow-striped braces. "How about these?"

"Fine." Then I asked, "What do you mean about my nose?"

"Stop," said Natalie, swinging her army satchel over her shoulder. "How do I look?"

"Great. Where are you going?"

"To the pub with Ava."

Ava's head snapped up. "You'd better not tell anyone."

"Think I'm stupid?" I bit my fingernail. "Can I come?"

"You're too young," Ava retorted as she stormed around getting ready.

"So's Natalie," I protested, but she turned up her nose. Natalie kept quiet, probably glad Ava let her come along.

I hoped and dreaded they'd get caught each time they went out, often coming out of my room late at night when I heard them bobbing down the hallway, reeking of fumes and cigarettes, their eyes half-closed, arms raggedy and thudding against the wall as they fell giggling and whispering into their room. For some reason, my parents never caught them. Once, my sisters landed at home to find my parents themselves giggling on the front steps, so drunk they didn't notice how out of their minds my sisters were. Natalie almost fell off her bed laughing about it the next day, the skin around her lips stretched tight like paper.

After my sisters left, I examined every inch of my face in the mirror, turning side to side to see whether I looked powerful or not. But all I saw was my nose taking up more than its fair share of the parking space. Scowling, I went back to my room to bury it in a book.

———

My mother coughed in the kitchen as she tried to light the gas stove.

"Where's Dad?" I asked, when she told me to set eight places instead of nine.

"He had to go away on business again." Her eyes were down as she peeled carrots. The back of her hands looked scaly. "He'll be back in a few days." Her voice sounded toneless. "He had to tie up a few things."

After supper, Natalie flounced off to her room. "I'm going out tonight."

She would be with Kevin again. Short with a pointy face, his fleshy lips looked blood red next to his pale skin, and he had lank brown hair over which he tied a yellow bandana. Natalie didn't laugh when I called him a wanker under my breath the first time we saw him ogling her through the school gates. He looked stupid fondling his motorbike.

"I can't believe he likes me," she said breathlessly when he asked her to go for a ride.

"Why not?" I scowled, jealous at the way her eyes lit up. "He's the lucky one."

Kevin said only one thing to me, and he said it every time he picked up Natalie. "Hullo there, ya wee pip-squeak," then he'd laugh and try to chuck me under the chin.

"Fuck off," I'd say, jerking away, but that only made him pat me on the head like he thought it was funny. Natalie scooted onto the backseat, grinning idiotically as they roared off.

"Where are you going?" I sulked now, sucking on a strand of hair.

Natalie buckled her army pants, then angled herself in front of the mirror and smeared kohl under her eyelids. "Nowhere."

"So why are you getting all dressed up?"

She looked around quickly, then slid over to shut the door. "I'm going to the Red Lion."

"Big deal. Is Ava going?"

"No, she's going out with David."

"You never let me come," I pouted.

"You can if you want," Natalie said casually, bending over to lace up her boots. "But don't let Mom catch you, that's all. I told her I'm going to Dino's for a get-together with some girls from school."

"A get-together," I snorted knowingly, then raced as fast as I could to my room to yank on my jeans before she changed her mind. My mother wasn't to know that Natalie hadn't been to Dino's for months and that she was never so corny as to say *get-together*.

We snuck out of the house while my mother was still in the kitchen putting away the dishes with her back to the door and ran to catch the bus. Down near Sauchiehall Street, Natalie and I pushed in the wooden doors of the Red Lion where Lounge was inscribed in fancy script on the glass panel. The facing door said Bar in thick capitals and was only for men, Natalie informed me. "Don't go in there or they'll think you're a prostitute," she warned.

The lounge was packed and steaming with smoke. A mountain of bodies swelled between booths hugging the walls. There was barely one inch of space anywhere. The drinkers looked happy, flushed, and sweaty, holding their woolen coats and corduroy jackets on their laps. The floor was covered in sawdust, and from the ceiling hung several brass candelabra glowing with electrical bulbs.

No one seemed to notice how young I was as, jumpy with excitement, I squeezed with Natalie against the bar counter. Natalie shouted her order of vodka and orange juice, then glanced at me and ordered another one. I waited for her at the back amid the throng as she went off to look for Kevin. I gulped my drink down, spluttering as it burned in my chest.

"Hullo, ya wee pip-squeak," a loud voice resounded in my ear. "Fancy seeing you here. Where's Natalie?"

"Fuck off," I said, pulling away from Kevin's beery slouch. "She's over there somewhere looking for you."

A man with round cheeks and black hair cascading down his shoulders stood beside Kevin. His face was so white it was almost yellow, and his lips were crimson and moist, like a cherry. He gazed at me with a half smile.

"Go on, introduce me," he shouted to Kevin over the din.

Kevin made a small bow in my direction. "Craig, Tosca, Tosca, Craig." He winked broadly at me. "See you later."

"What are you drinking?" Craig asked.

I awkwardly pulled my hair across my face to curtain my blush. "Vodka," I stammered.

"Straight up? It'll put the hair on your chest."

I giggled. "Yeah."

"Right, then. I'll be back." He sauntered off. His black jeans fit his plump body so tightly that I could see the round bulge where his backside turned into his thigh. His flannel shirt was tucked in over his soft-looking back. I bit my lip, scared I was about to be made a fool of. What if he didn't come back? I downed the rest of my drink.

Natalie watched me from the bar where she'd met up with Kevin. A slightly hunched man stood beside her, dressed in a brown leather jacket and jeans. His long brown hair drooped in a straight line down his back.

"That was McCrystal, a friend of Ava's," Natalie told me later. "He's fancied Ava for ages, but Ava's more interested in David."

Natalie moved closer to Kevin as he waved a ten-shilling note over the bar to buy more drinks. She cocked her head at me and mouthed something, her glasses glittering with the reflection of the overhead lights.

"What?" I mouthed back, feeling slightly unsteady.

She shook her head and turned back to Kevin.

I tried to lean nonchalantly against the wall like I was a regular, peeking through my hair at the mass of bodies thickening between me and the bar to see if Craig was coming back. I jolted when I felt a nudge on my right.

"Oh, hi," I said casually, my cheeks burning.

Craig pulled me by the hand to the nearest booth. "Come

on, there's a space here." He cocked his head at two women who had piled their bags and coats in the wide gap between them. "Do you mind?"

They rolled their eyes and reluctantly heaped their stuff on the floor. He sat on the bench beside me, so close I could smell the earthy scent of his hair. He downed half of his pint, then wiped the foam of his beer off his upper lip. "You have a beautiful name."

I took a tiny sip of my vodka. "Thank you."

He put his hand on the table next to mine. His fingers were short and squat, with little dimples around the knuckles. "Are you American?" His eyes widened, like he was impressed. He flipped open his pack of cigarettes and offered me one, then struck a match on the table top, winking at me when he caught my startled expression.

"Are you on holiday?"

"No." I giggled, clammy under my sweater. "I live here."

"Really? What do you do?"

I dragged on my cigarette, a cold thread of nervousness running through the warm wooziness of the vodka.

"Um . . . I . . . er . . ." I said, smoke put-putting from between my lips.

"It's okay, I'm only having you on," he said with a wink. He took another swig of his pint. "Kevin told me about you."

"He did?" I puffed hard on my cigarette and kept my tone casual. "What did he say?"

"Nothing much. Just that you and Natalie are always

tagging about together. He likes you. He says you're funny."

"I thought he hated me," I blurted, then broke into giggles.

"What are you laughing at?" said Craig.

"I don't know," I gulped, trying to quell the nervous laughter rippling through me.

Craig slipped his arm around me. It felt heavy and gentle on my shoulders. "Can I walk you home?" he murmured. His cheek lay close to my mouth.

"I don't know," I honked, hiding my face in my hair.

"Please," he said teasingly, pulling away. He lifted a lock of my hair and twisted it around his finger.

"Do you really want to?" I glanced sideways at him.

"Aye, I do," he said.

"Okay," I answered shyly.

"Do what you want," Natalie said stonily when I passed by and told her I was leaving. She looked like she was in the middle of a fight with Kevin, who stared angrily at the row of liquor bottles behind the bar.

It had begun raining again. Craig removed his jacket and held it over our heads as we tripped toward Byres Road. When he put his arm around me, I wrapped mine hesitatingly around his waist. His breath felt warm on my cheek as he leaned down to kiss me.

"It's so cold tonight," I said to cover up my shiver of excitement.

Craig gently gathered up my hair to pull me closer. I raised my face. Then his lips were on mine, thin and cold and moist.

His tongue poked between my lips, trying to draw them apart. I pulled away to gasp in air. Craig tilted my chin up with his forefinger.

"You can breathe through your nose," he said cheerfully. He chuckled like he thought I was adorable. When his mouth pressed into mine again, I drew my lips apart and floated along with him, my breasts pressing into his soft chest, hands reaching up to feel the smooth texture of his neck. He slid his arms down my back and wrapped me against him as rain fell softly on our faces.

"You're gorgeous," he whispered, caressing the back of my head.

"So are you," I panted, looking up at him in ecstasy.

"Come on," he said softly, lifting his soaked jacket back up over our heads. "Let's get you home before you catch your death."

At my corner, I said reluctantly, "I'd better go."

"When can I see you again?" he asked. His lips tickled my ear. "You could come to my bedsit. I live off the Motherwell Road. I could meet you after school."

"Yes," I breathed, delirious with joy. After a last kiss, I floated up the stairs and into my room, barely noticing my mother had already gone to bed and didn't care that I was back minus Natalie, or that Ava was still out.

When I heard Natalie creeping down the hallway, I stole to her room and told her about Craig. "He's so amazing, he told me he wanted to see me again, he—"

"That's great," she answered absently.

"He told me I'm beautiful," I continued confidentially. I frowned, suddenly worried. "Do you think he was just saying that?" I turned on the light and examined myself anxiously in the mirror. I smoothed down my hair. Then I wrapped my arms around myself and whirled around, making the wardrobe shudder as I banged into it.

"He's so incredible," I breathed.

"Turn off the light," said Natalie grumpily, slipping under the bedcovers.

Have you done it before?" Craig whispered, his breath frosting the air. The blanket covering his bed was musty pink, checkered with maroon stripes, and his curtains drawn across the wide squares of the window were green with yellow flowers. He pulled my shirt over my head, then lifted me onto the bed while I giggled. With a click the small, electric one-bar fire barely heating the room went dark as the electric meter ran out.

"No," I shivered, the sheets icy beneath me. I rolled on my side and wrapped my arm around his chest, burrowing my nose in his neck. He smelled like Fairy Liquid and milk.

"Neither have I." He unsnapped my bra and cupped my breast awkwardly in his hand.

He leaned across and kissed me. Then he rolled on top of me, taking off his shirt first. His body felt soft and squishy. I squirmed nervously and stroked his hair from my face to stop it tickling my nose.

He was arched upward to take out his penis. I snuck a look. I gasped. It looked like a big red flashlight.

"How's it going to fit?" I squeaked. I thought a penis was the size of a worm, like Rock's when I'd caught him peeing in the backyard.

"I don't know," he said uncertainly. His penis felt as thick and hard as a truncheon along the inside of my thigh.

"Are you sure?" he whispered.

"Yes," I answered with false bravado. I thrashed about with his heavy weight on me, trying to open my legs wide enough for him to come in. I closed my eyes, trying not to think about how big it was. I put my hand down to guide it. It was fleshy and rubbery in my hand as I angled it toward my opening. Suddenly Craig gave a push, and a scream escaped from my mouth. I felt like I was going to rip in half.

"Are you all right? I love you," Craig panted in my ear, his back awash in sweat. "I love you so much. You're the best thing that ever happened to me."

"I love you, too," I lied, burning between my legs. I noticed a strip of wallpaper had leaked off the wall. Was this it? I thought. What everyone was always talking about, what my father had warned me about, my mother's chin in the air whenever she saw anyone kissing in the street? Big deal. But I turned my face toward Craig when he leaned to kiss me, and lifted my hands from under the warm covers to fondle the back of his head. So what if it didn't feel like anything? A boy liked me, even if he was nineteen and I was thirteen. How easy it was.

"When can I see you again?" Craig nuzzled my neck as I left him on the corner near my house. "Can I see you tomorrow?" He squeezed me tightly and kissed me all over my face.

"Soon," I answered vaguely. There must be something wrong with him if he liked me this much, I thought. I didn't turn back as I walked painfully down the street.

ater that night the phone echoed shrilly. The police were on the line, informing my parents that Natalie had been picked up blind drunk in George Square. Kevin was no longer a minor so he was being kept in a cell overnight until he sobered up.

My father answered calmly, "We'll come and get her. I'm sure there's been some kind of mistake."

In the hallway, my mother's voice was strained, angry. "I'm going to kill her if she said anything. How dare she get picked up like that."

My father's voice sounded soothing in comparison though I could tell it was only to reassure her. "She doesn't know anything."

By the time my parents arrived at the police station, Natalie was scared sober. She started crying when she saw them. She told me about it later, her eyes woodenly staring ahead and lips twisted in bitterness.

"I'm sorry," she'd sobbed, trying to put her head down on my mother's breast. My mother's chin rose in the air as she turned to thank the police inspector. My father smiled and shook the officer's hand.

"She won't be bothering you again, sir," he said.

On the way home, my father parked on a side street and yanked Natalie by the hair out of the car. "How dare you," he hissed and punched Natalie into the gutter. "How dare you jeopardize us like that?" He kicked her again and again as my sister lay choking over a sewer drain.

My mother laid a hand on my father's arm. "Stop," she said. "You'll break her glasses. They were expensive." She reached down and removed them from my sister's face.

Natalie said she wished she been kept in jail. "At least the police didn't hit me." Her arms and legs were stained blue where my father had punched and kicked her. Her eyes were so puffy from crying she could hardly open them. "They won't let me see Kevin anymore," she whimpered.

The next night, she woke me with a hand over my mouth. "Promise you won't tell anyone," she whispered. "I'm running away." In the faint light leaking through the curtains, she looked ghostly.

"Can I come with you?"

She shook her head vehemently. "No."

"Why can't I come, too? It's not fair."

"Shh! You'll wake everyone up." Drawing her face close to

mine, she said, "Don't tell anyone and I'll let you join me later. I'm going to Edinburgh. Kevin said we could stay with his sister."

"Promise?" I asked anxiously, a pit of fear in my stomach.

"I promise," she whispered.

"Where is she?" my father snarled at breakfast. All eyes swung to my face, except Ava's. She turned to the window, humming under her breath. My spine tingled, but I kept coolly spooning cereal into my mouth.

"You'd better tell him, Tosca," my mother warned, pouring my father's coffee from cup to cup so it wouldn't burn his lips.

"Who me?"

"Don't you 'who me.' Where is she?" My father slapped his hand on the table.

"I don't know. Honest, I don't."

My father turned his palms upward. "I'm so worried about her," he said. His eyes were pools of blue. "It's dangerous out there. You don't want anything to happen to her, do you?"

The words tumbled out of my mouth. "She went to Edinburgh." Before I could blink, the blue had hardened into gray and he was on his feet.

"Let's go," he called to my mother who was already at the front door.

"What have I done?" I wailed alone in my room. Maybe Natalie won't know it was me, I thought in a panic. Maybe she'll think my parents found out by themselves.

"It's okay," she responded in a subdued voice when I told

her how sorry I was after they dragged her back home. She wouldn't come out of her room for two days, and when she did, her gait was stiff and her eyes blank.

"I would have done the same thing. There was nothing else you could do, he's a bastard." She gazed into the distance, her face dry and colorless. She paused, then continued, pulling her fingers so hard they cracked, her knuckles red and raw looking. "Dad said I can't see Kevin anymore." Her voice sounded leaden. "I have to come home straight from school. I can't go out anymore."

Kevin turned up at school, and he and Natalie whispered into each other's mouths while I stood by trembling with fear. I nudged my sister, urging it was time to go before we got caught.

She walked home with her head bowed. "I wish Kevin understood," she said, kicking a stone out of her way. "He has no fucking idea about Dad."

"I know what you fucking mean," I said, glancing around quickly before lighting a cigarette and smoking it behind my cupped palm.

My mother ran down the stairs after my father. "Who could that be at this time of night?" Her voice was taut with worry. Branches slapped against one another in the moonless sky, cracking sharply in the wind.

"Be quiet, will you?" my father's low voice echoed up the stairs.

Through the door below stood a short fat man clutching a thick envelope. My father's eyes narrowed before he fixed a grin on his face.

"Why Mike," he said swinging the door open. "How nice to see you. What are you doing in these parts?"

Clean-shaven, the man smiled without showing his teeth. "Hello, Aaron, glad to see you're here."

My father ushered him in and led him upstairs. I didn't move fast enough to avoid my mother's sharp look when she caught me watching.

"Get the hell away from here," she hissed.

Mike sidled beside her and leaned closely into my face. "Which daughter is this? Ava? Natalie? Marilyn?"

My father eased next to him, barely making eye contact with me, and led him away. "You should be in bed," he said to me in a clipped, polite tone.

Mike, still grinning with his lips sealed, let my father steer him into the living room. After the door closed, my mother became glued to the carpet in the frosty hallway. "I don't know why there's got to be all this trouble," she said tensely to herself. "Why can't he just pay people off like everyone else does? They do him a favor, and he's got to be Mr. Big all over again."

She twisted the ring on her finger. "Now we're going to have to move again. You'll see, you just wait and see." She disappeared into their bedroom, muttering away.

There was no point in peeping through the keyhole as my

father had sealed it with putty right after we moved in, so I went back to bed filled with dread.

In the morning, the hallway was pungent with the smell of bacon and eggs and toast. The living room was empty. I crept into the kitchen to find my mother adorned with sunglasses and turbaned in a terry-cloth towel, the cloth stained with welts of nail polish. She scraped a knife beneath the bacon in the teflon pan as Rock kicked Fig under the table and Marilyn cried. She kept on scraping until the bacon was covered in black dots while her lips worked silently.

"Where's Dad?" I asked nervously.

Kirk's head snapped up, his eyes wide and dark, but he only blinked and chewed his bottom lip. Natalie snorted she didn't give a shite where I found her sitting on the floor of her bedroom with a huge sketchbook open in her lap. Her fingers were smudged black from the series of figures she was drawing in charcoal, their outlines growing darker as they huddled together in an increasingly dusky sky.

My father reappeared that night with the usual spring in his step and smelling fresh. But the next day I accidentally walked in on him in the living room, looking for my schoolbook, and found him sitting in the dark by the window, drinking out of a large glass. A half-empty bottle of Johnnie Walker sat on the table beside him.

"S-s-sorry," I stammered, backing out of the room and closing the door behind me with a tiny click.

"Where's Dad?" I asked Natalie the next morning when my father wasn't anywhere to be seen.

"What are you asking me for?" Natalie's voice was mixed with boredom.

"God, sorry," I said, aggrieved.

Ava sat at the edge of her bed staring mutely at the floor, not seeming to notice we were there. She kept thrusting up a hand to push her hair off her face.

I squinted at her suspiciously as she emptied her side of the wardrobe into a suitcase. With a determined look, she walked around me and went back to her side of the room. She slipped her hand under her mattress and pulled out a wad of pound notes. After shoving them in her purse and picking up her suitcase, she pushed past me into the hallway. She blanched as she ran into my mother.

"I'm leaving," she said emphatically.

My mother's head swiveled. "You're what? What are you talking about?"

"You heard me. I'm not staying in this lunatic asylum. You can't stop me," Ava taunted. "I'm eighteen." She tossed her head. "And anyway, David said I could move in with him."

"David? That little pushover? Don't you think you can do better than that?"

"Don't you dare talk about him like that!" Ava railed.

"And just how do you think you're going to manage?" My mother's eyes glinted. "You can't expect Dad to pay the bills."

Ava snorted. "I've got my own money. I work," she said defiantly.

They faced each other, both of their faces tightening into white masks of hatred.

My mother's eyes rolled darkly. "You just wait until Dad gets back. Boy, are you in for it this time."

A sarcastic look crossed Ava's face. Her grin was pure spite. "You don't know for sure if he's coming back and you know it."

"What are you talking about?" my mother barked. "Of course he's coming back. You don't know anything, so you'd better just shut that mouth of yours if you know what's good for you."

"Fuck you," said Ava.

My mother's hand rose to hit her, then she spun around and stomped into the living room.

"Why, where is he?" I asked Ava irately.

"Are you really going?" said Kirk, fascinated as he came out of the kitchen with a half-eaten sandwich.

"What do you think?" Ava retorted.

"Where are you going?" He seemed impressed.

"As far fucking away as I can."

"Are you really going to live with David?" I asked.

My mother appeared in the hallway and blocked Ava's exit. "I talked to Dad," she said. "He said you can't go. He won't allow it. He's going to be back in a few days, and then you'll see."

"What's for him to allow?" snarled Ava. "He has no choice."

I had never seen my mother so angry. "You can't go!" she shrieked. "I won't let you."

My sister brushed her aside, her face ashen. "Mom, I'm warning you. There's nothing you can do." She slammed down the suitcase. "I never wanted to come here in the first place," she yelled. "You and Dad think you can do whatever you want. Well, you can't. I'm leaving."

She grabbed her case and raced down the hallway and through the front door.

My mother stood rigidly in the hallway, fist raised. Suddenly a look of disinterest washed over her face. "Good riddance to bad rubbish," she said.

"Can I move in with Natalie?" I asked quickly.

After a pause, my mother answered in a cold, methodical voice. "Yes, go ahead."

I ran in and told Natalie gleefully that our mother said I could move in.

The indifference in Natalie's voice took the wind out of my sails. "Do what you want."

I'd barely woken up the next morning when Ava appeared by my bedside with a pinched face.

"That was fast," she said angrily.

"Mom said I could," I stammered guiltily.

"Get the fuck out of my bed," she answered, yanking off the bedcovers.

"What happened?" Natalie called from the other side of the room.

"David said I couldn't stay with him."

"What a fucking idiot. Why not?"

Ava sounded furious. "He said Dad was going to kill him if he found out we were living together without being married. I broke up with him."

"Oh, Christ," said Natalie, her face creased. "Can't you just get married?"

"No, I can't," Ava said coldly, and started throwing her things back into the wardrobe.

L et's get some fags," I said with forced amiability to Natalie on the way to school, scared she hated me as much as Ava did for moving into her room so fast. I kept out of Ava's way the rare times she was home.

"Sure." As we walked slowly down the street she mumbled miserably, "I think Ava's stupid for not just getting a bedsit. She's lucky she's old enough to get away." We traipsed into O'Connor's.

"Ten Woodbines," Natalie said casually after passing through the green doorway.

"And we don't want them untipped this time," I piped up.

I gestured at the shelf behind the barrel-chested shop owner. Mr. O'Connor's rolled-up sleeves revealed a blue and red tattoo that read "Sweets for My Sweet" inside a heart. He had told Natalie and me that he got it in the army as a present for his girlfriend.

"You're from America?" he had asked the first time we'd come in. "I have an aunt in Cleveland, Ohio. Do you know her?"

I didn't even know where Cleveland was.

"Those ones," I pointed again. "The ones with the filters."

Natalie and I dug into our pockets for coins. Suddenly, a large hand appeared on the counter from behind and picked up the cigarettes.

"I'll take those," said my father. Just as abruptly as he had appeared, he vanished, making the bell on the door ring loudly.

Natalie and I turned to one another in panic. My father was the only person who could be here and gone at the same time.

"I'm sorry, girls," said Mr. O'Connor sounding worried as he came out from behind the counter. "I don't want any trouble. You're not to come here anymore." He raised his hands and shooed us away. "Keep your money. Tell your father I thought they were for him."

After a terrified day at school, Natalie and I walked home together trying to guess what our punishment would be. As we turned off Hyndland Road, smoke blew thick and fast out of an alleyway and out flew Rock and another boy covered in black ash.

"What the hell are you doing?" demanded Natalie.

"Nothing. It wasn't us." Rock giggled, and then took off in

the direction away from home, waving a box of matches in the dank air. A cardboard box that they must have set on fire smoldered at the back of the houses.

"Fucking pyromaniacs," wheezed Natalie.

My father's car sat in the driveway. Even from there we could hear my mother screeching in their bedroom above, not caring if anyone could hear her.

"Do you know what my life is like? Do you even give a damn?" After a silence, she yelled, "Ava treats me like a dog, Tosca's always talking back to me, I caught Natalie telling Kevin on the phone that she's going to move in with him, the boys wrote all over their walls with black marker, and all you can say is you're sorry?"

"I should have never let Ava get a job," my father retorted. "It set a bad example."

My mother's voice hardened as I eavesdropped outside their bedroom door. "Did you tell anyone anything?"

"Of course not, what do you think I am?" My father sounded irritated and lit a cigarette with the whish of his lighter. "Anyway, I told you a thousand times. It's all over. They're not going to be bothering me anymore."

I could hear my mother's nails tapping the glass on her vanity table. "I don't want to ask how you managed to do that."

"I keep telling you not to worry. All they needed was some grease. Mike's just a message boy. That's all they were after."

"What's a message boy?" I whispered to Natalie, relieved my

father seemed to have forgotten all about O'Connor's and the Woodbines.

She raised her eyebrows and motioned for me to keep quiet.

Something caught in my mother's voice. "I'm sick of this. So now we're going to be able to forget all about it and live like normal people?"

My father didn't answer. Then he said in a mild voice, "I said they won't be bothering us anymore. I took care of it."

My mother's voice rose, aggrieved. "What about the kids? You think the way they're acting is normal?"

My father cleared his throat. "I'll deal with it. Happy now?"

She spluttered. "Happy?" she said scathingly. "I know what would make me happy. That you take me on some of your business trips."

"Okay, I'll see what I can do," my father answered calmly.

My father knocked on my bedroom door the next morning while I played the guitar Kevin had given Natalie. I didn't hear him at first and gave a start when he opened the door.

"Tosca, could you come here for a moment?"

I put down the instrument apprehensively and followed him out. Waving me onto the couch, he sat down and played with his cigarette holder. I fidgeted, planning to say the cigarettes he'd caught us buying were going to be a present for him. He cleared his throat.

"How would you like to be as pretty as, say, Janet Leigh?"

"Who's she?"

He grimaced. "The actress in that movie you never saw," he

said sarcastically. "The point is how would you like to be pretty? How would you like to have a nose job?"

"A nose job?"

"You know, have your nose straightened." Tap-tap, and he inserted a cigarette into his shiny black holder.

I stared at him, stunned, fear tingling in my stomach. My father's face came back into focus.

"Hello, are you still with me?"

"I don't want a different nose," I said. Outside the window, the branches of the tall oak tree waved back and forth. A thin curl of smoke rose from my father's cigarette.

"Don't be difficult. I'm only trying to help. Mommy told me that the kids at school call you Beaky. Don't you think it's reasonable for you to do something about it?"

"They call Kirk Girl, but you're not going to make him change, are you?" I asked.

"Don't be fresh, young lady." My father glared at me. "You might not know this, but I'm concerned about your welfare. I'll have you know when I was in London, I took time out from my busy schedule to discuss you with a specialist. He agrees that you should have it done, while you're thirteen, before you stop developing. I even made an appointment for you!" He sounded indignant. "Don't you think a little gratitude is in order?"

"But I don't want a different nose," I said tremulously.

My father's face lost the rumpled appearance he usually had in the mornings before his coffee, before he pieced himself together with starch, hair cream, and aftershave.

"You're not being reasonable," he said in exasperation. "This is for your own good. What about when you get older and start looking for a husband? Do you think anyone is going to want you?" He squashed out his cigarette and chuckled to himself. "They'll call you Nosy Parker. Miss Nosy Parker, the old spinster who sticks her nose into everything."

"They can call me whatever they want!"

My father's eyes passed over me as if he had lost interest. He shrugged. "It's your life. Just don't come to me later and ask me to pay for one because it'll be too late."

A few days later, my father came to me again, this time while I was on my bed, reading a book. He stood before me, hands folded. "Did you give my suggestion further thought?"

"You mean about my nose?" I shook my head. "I don't want it done. I told you the first time."

"Don't you talk back to me, you—" He took a breath. "So, you've decided you don't want to be pretty. Madame Tosca here has decided that—"

"I don't want to look like anyone else," I protested. "I want to look like me."

My father raised his eyebrows. "You win," he said, sounding surprised. "Just forget about it. It's for your own welfare." He shrugged. "If you don't want my help, what can I do?"

Natalie and my father disappeared into the living room after dinner. Then a knock sounded on my door, and Natalie appeared in my bedroom. Her hands trembled as she pressed them together.

"Tosca," she began hesitatingly, avoiding my eyes. "Don't you think it would be a good idea to get a nose job? I mean, wouldn't you be happier that way?"

"Are you kidding?" I sat up, ready to laugh.

"No, I mean it. Would it really be so horrible?"

"What are you talking about?"

Natalie's lips quivered. "If you agree to do it, Dad will let me leave home. He said I can't unless you have your nose fixed."

I looked at her, aghast.

Natalie wrung her hands. "Please do it. I can't take it anymore. I just can't." Her lips were covered in white specks. "Please, Tosca."

She looked so pale, so gaunt, a blue bandana wrapped around her thin throat, her flat stomach a slight curve beneath the cotton shirt tucked into her army pants, the wide canvas belt encircling her waist, her clunky brown army boots. In a daze, I remembered the bruises on her arms and legs after my parents had brought her back from Edinburgh, so many more bruises than when she'd been arrested in George Square. If it hadn't been for me, she would already be free. It was my fault she'd gotten caught.

The thoughts ticked mechanically across my brow as I sat cross-legged on the floor across from her. Suddenly I felt perfectly reasonable and calm, just as my father had asked me to be. My voice drifted into the space between us. "Okay, I'll do it."

"You will?" Natalie's gasp of joy made my chest crack.

"Thank you! Oh, thank you, thank you!" Her hands pressed into mine, making my fingers jump up and down along with hers.

Long after she was gone from the room, I lay numbly on the floor in the darkness. I was so ugly I had to change my face. Even Natalie said so. It wasn't a secret anymore. The whole world knew. I'd tried to hide it, hanging my hair over my face like a curtain, but all along everyone could see it, that big ugly monstrosity in the middle of my face. It was so ugly it had to be chopped off.

On the plane to London, alone with my father, the stewardess's face appeared in a blur after we took off. She grinned prettily at him, her nose straight and small, her tiny red lips like a rosebud as she poured him a whisky. Why doesn't he ever look at me like that? I thought bitterly as he smiled back warmly, and I turned away to stare blindly out the window.

Our first stop was Moorgate in the financial district, where my father carried out an hour appointment while I waited in the back of the cab. On the street, men in black suits and hats and women with ankle-length coats scurried to and fro. The buildings were old but not gray like in Glasgow, and the red brick added color to the street. No one glanced my way or noticed that the cab had been in the same place with the motor running for so long.

"This won't take long. I have another meeting to get to," my father said cheerfully as he held open the door for me to the nose doctor's office on Harley Street a few miles away. The office smelled of wood, the walls paneled in rich mahogany squares.

"Good afternoon, Mr. Rung," smiled the doctor, dressed in a pin-striped suit and red tie. Above his etched jaw lay rows of even white teeth. It was his nose, though, that caught my attention. It was one of those noses that was so long, it didn't have anywhere to go but sideways. It made Doctor Fortuna seem off-center, odd, as if his face were about to fall over.

"This must be Tosca," he said. "What a lovely name." He parted my hair and placed two hands on my cheeks. "Oh, yes," he said, checking my nose as he turned my face to the left and the right and then to the left again. "I see what you mean. This is a rather—heh-heh—striking nose."

I jerked my head away. Doctor Fortuna and my father exchanged a knowing look.

"It's the age," said the doctor. "I have two of my own." He moved to his desk and pulled out a portfolio, much like a photograph album, only larger. "Have a look at these, Tosca. You can choose the one you want." He opened the portfolio to pages of little boxed-in noses, cut small so that there were eight on every sheet. Each one was covered in plastic. There were short ones, stubby ones, bony ones, fleshy ones, ones like my father's—straight with just the right amount of skin—and ones like my mother's—slightly upturned and with a pointy tip. Then there were the nostrils—slender, delicate, refined or thick, or open and flaring on either side in perfect symmetry.

"How about this one?" suggested Dr. Fortuna. "It'll go nicely with your eyes. Or that one? Petite, feminine."

"Okay." My voice floated above me, dismembered.

My father dropped me off at the hospital and flew back to Glasgow. I stayed in a private room in the hospital for three days as Doctor Fortuna said I needed time to heal before I could risk any movement.

"The slightest nudge could damage the setting," he said after the operation when he poked around at the large bandage. My eyes were so swollen and my head so full, he seemed like an apparition floating above me. "Make sure you don't bump into anything."

On the third day after the operation, I rode to the airport in a taxi my father had ordered, sealed in the back, trying to hide my face so no one could see me with my black eyes and bandaged nose. I kept my eyes down at the airport and on the plane. Natalie came out to the hallway when I arrived home.

"Tosca," she cried, looking scared.

"Hi," I replied dully.

"Why are you all black and blue?"

"From the operation," I mumbled. The bandage made it difficult to talk.

As she hugged me my nose banged into her shoulder.

"Oh, shit!" she yelped when my nose started dripping blood.

"Give me a tissue," I said, stemming the flow with my sleeve. "And stop staring at me."

———

A few days after my fourteenth birthday, Natalie came to my room. "Tosca, I have a present for you."

"What is it?" I asked, barely looking up from my book.

In her hands was the guitar that Kevin had given her, with a painted mural depicting a blue and green ocean with iridescent goldfish swimming just below the surface. "Here, it's yours."

I turned it over in my hands. "Are you sure?" I asked hesitantly.

She exhaled, as if relieved, and smiled. "Yeah, I painted it for you. Do you like it?"

"Yeah," I exclaimed, surprised back into a feeling of warmth. "Wow, thanks!"

She sat down. "I wanted to tell you before anyone else. Kevin and I are getting married."

I choked, "You're what?"

She calmly removed her glasses to clean them on her plaid shirt. "Dad found out I was going to move in with Kevin. He told me I have to get married or he won't let me leave home."

"What a fucking bastard," I said. "What a fucking bastard." I started crying. "After all that."

Her brow furrowed. "After all what?"

I blinked at her uncomprehendingly through my tears. "You told me to get my nose fixed so you could leave home."

"What are you talking about? You always said your nose was too big. You look better now."

"Really?" I asked uncertainly, confused. "You think so?"

"Yeah, sure. Anyway, the wedding is going to be soon, so I can get the fuck out of here."

"Yeah," I echoed flatly. "That'll be great."

Are you sure?" he whispered, lying down beside me on the bed upstairs. "Kevin told me you're only fourteen." His face looked shiny in the glow of the streetlight through the window.

"I've done it before," I retorted.

Kevin's friend, Matthew, had arrived late to Natalie's engagement party downstairs at Kevin's parents' house, and made straight for the row of whisky and vodka bottles on the coffee table. I'd hardly seen my sister since she'd made her announcement. Matthew had asked me to dance and then come upstairs with him. I said yes, just so I could get away from seeing Natalie cuddling in Kevin's arms.

The party was still going on downstairs. Kevin's parents had taken off for the pub. Mine had gone home, my mother covering her ears and saying she couldn't stand the noise, it gave her a headache.

Matthew's wavy orange hair fell over his forehead when he bent to kiss me. "You're pretty."

"No, I'm not," I said mechanically. The music pounded

through the floor beneath the drunken laughter. Matthew's fingers grazed the sides of my body.

"You're sure you've done it before?"

"Yes," I said, shifting my legs so he could take my panties off.

The music grew louder, making something rattle on the vanity table. Boom-boom. Boom-boo-boo-boom. When he was done, Matthew rolled over and stood up to switch on the light. "Let's go dance," he said cheerily. "I'll get us a drink."

The light made my eyes hurt. "Okay," I said woodenly. I bunched up my tights and shoved them in my pocket, then stood at the bottom of the stairs waiting for Matthew to come back. But when I saw Kevin and Natalie happily dancing, I headed for home.

Natalie got married two weeks later and moved into a flat near Kelvingrove Park that she and Kevin bought with my father's wedding gift of a down payment. The day of the wedding I locked myself in the bathroom and refused to come out. After I heard the front door slam with my mother shouting, "Leave her then," I tried to yank the nose off my face. I worked my way down, hitting myself, punching my arms and legs until they were covered in bruises.

Barely three weeks after the wedding, while my mother was ordering me to stop looking so miserable and help her serve lunch, my father appeared in the kitchen, rubbing his hands.

"It's all set. We'll be moving to London in a week."

"Why are we going to London?" said Kirk crossly. "What's wrong with it here?"

My father laughed. "Why, I'm opening an office. Mr. McKenzie sold out his half of the company, and London is a better location for expanding the business."

"What kind of business?" Fig piped up.

"That's very courteous of you, Fig. Thanks for offering to help get the suitcases down."

"Uh," stuttered Fig in confusion.

I clattered the plates on the table and ran blindly out of the kitchen to the phone.

"Natalie's not here," said Kevin. "She's at the doctor's, having a flap of skin removed from her throat. She won't be able to talk for a bit."

"You're lying. Let me talk to her, you bastard," I shouted, the receiver clenched in my grip.

"Don't be so stupid," he said. Shhtuupit. "I wouldn't lie about a thing like that."

"If you're so smart, tell me how a piece of skin can grow in your throat!" I spit into the phone.

His voice sounded calm. "Listen, Tosca, I know you're upset about something, but don't take it out on me, all right?"

I banged the heavy black phone so hard the veneer of the table cracked. Then I held up the receiver and bellowed, "Tell her we're moving to London."

With the radio on so loud, my mother didn't hear me and hummed as she unhooked pictures in the living room. She'd lost weight and looked slim and chipper in her new sweater dress as I ran by and slammed my bedroom door.

Ava coolly removed the last of her things from the flat and informed my father that she wasn't coming with us. He didn't threaten her or argue but instead turned his back and walked out of the room as if she were no more than a closed chapter.

"Where are you going?" I spluttered, jealous she could leave.

"None of your business," she said, tossing her head in the air.

I snuck over to the Red Lion the afternoon before we left to see if I could find Matthew, but he was nowhere to be found. A bearded man with long black hair called John bought me a drink, and as we guzzled down one Newcastle Brown Ale after the other, he leaned over the table, thin arms dangling by his sides, and asked me if I wanted to go to his place.

I grabbed my duffle coat off the back of the chair, making the wooden togs clack together. "Sure."

John raised his brow in glee, as if he'd expected me to say no. "All right, then."

He stood so tall, my neck hurt when he kissed me at the bus stop. We entered his flat and walked straight into a room with a bed. A woman in a patchwork skirt quilted in lime green and brown squares sat at its edge, poking a needle into her forearm.

"Go easy," John said to her. "Some of that's mine." With a grin in my direction, he said, "Take a pew. I'll make you a cup of tea."

"It's okay. I don't want any."

I examined the woman, fascinated by the line of blood oozing down her arm. With a dazed expression, she pulled down her sleeve and swayed slightly as she came to her feet.

"Oh, sorry," she said thickly, her hooded eyes sweeping between John and me. "I'll be out of your way."

"Is that your girlfriend?" I asked nervously after she disappeared behind a door paned with oblique glass.

"No, that's only Heather," he said.

He sat at the sink fixed into the wall and dipped some brown powder onto a tablespoon, then added water and cooked it for a few moments with his lighter. After picking up the syringe the woman had been using, he loaded it with the mixture.

I watched in curiosity as he rolled up the sleeve of his flannel shirt, tied a leather belt around his upper arm, and bit hard on the end with his teeth. He tapped the vein in the crook of his elbow, then poked in the needle and kept it in until a trickle of blood shot into it, a spurt of watery red. Clenching his teeth, he pressed the plunger slow and hard. He waited for a moment before letting the strap go with a rush. His head fell back, his Adam's apple on its end like a triangle, while the syringe dangled in his slack forearm.

I stayed motionless, wondering if I should go. It was getting cold. My watch read only four o'clock. I didn't feel like going home yet. A crash resounded from the next room, like someone had dropped a pot or a frying pan.

"Fuck," a man yelled.

John lurched over and threw up into the sink.

"Are you okay?" I asked tentatively.

He nodded, wiping his mouth on his sleeve. "I'm all right." He proffered the syringe. "Want a hit?"

I shuddered. "No, thanks."

His hair smelled like chips, and after he sat beside me on the bed, his hands easily explored my body. We rolled around kissing, and I panted like I was enjoying it.

"I'm moving to London tomorrow," I said as he slipped his hand into my panties.

"Are you?" he said in a muffled voice. "That's a shame, us just getting to know each other."

He drew me off the bed. "Come with me," he said, his fingers twitching in mine. He led me into the bathroom. "We'd better go in here in case someone comes wandering in."

We lay down on the floor with the cold black and white tiles seeping into my back, and I writhed and humped in what I thought were all the right places until he let out a long, wavering sigh and flopped down on top of me.

"Do you like me?" I whispered.

"Aye," he mumbled, and soon started snoring.

A little while later, I angled away from under his sleeping body and let myself out.

I landed back home to my bath night, my last bath night in

Scotland, and as I lay in the hot water with the radio perched on the rim I listened to a repeat of "Desert Island Discs" because there was nothing else on. I twisted the volume button louder and louder until my father banged on the door and yelled at me to turn it down or I'd be in big trouble.

When we had arrived in Scotland, we'd had nine suitcases, two photograph albums, and one family portrait. We had been all together, including Ava and Natalie, who felt the same way about my parents as I did. Now we were seven, and I had never felt so alone.

CHAPTER NINE

LONDON TOWN

My mother and father had already disappeared into
their cabin when I boarded the train for London.
Rock and Fig ran up and down the narrow corridor,
opening and slamming shut the compartment doors. Raising
my guitar up high, I pretended I didn't know them and edged
into the cabin marked on my ticket.

The cabin was narrow, with only two bunks and a minia-
ture sink with a hairspray-speckled mirror overhead. Marilyn
blinked at me from the lower bunk.

"Are we there yet?" she asked sleepily.

"No," I said, hurling my suitcase on my bunk. "Go to sleep.
We'll get there faster that way."

"Hey, Tosca, what happened to your nose?" she asked un-
expectedly.

"What do you mean?"

"Mommy said you went to the hospital."

"Oh that." I crouched on her bed. "See this?" I put my fingers on my nose and wiggled it from side to side. "It's made of putty. No one can touch it or it'll change shape."

She gaped at me, wide-eyed.

"So you'd better be a good girl and do what Daddy says or else your nose might turn into putty, too."

Marilyn disappeared under the covers so fast, her pillow toppled to the floor. Snorting bitterly, I picked it up. "Go back to sleep."

I angled against the sink and lowered the window. A guard in a dark blue uniform piled luggage into the middle of the train. A woman hugged a young man good-bye, handing him a package wrapped in colorful wrapping paper as a whistle shrilled in the night air.

"Everybody aboard!" shouted the conductor.

From far away, a man yelled, "Stop! Wait!" but the train had already jolted forward. His arms waved frantically, but soon he turned into a dot as we picked up speed out of the station.

After I turned off the switch, streetlights flickered like stripes against the window as the train chugged past houses and shops, my sisters, and three years of my life. I squinted into the dark, throbbing with loneliness. As the train swung sharply to the side a baby started crying next door.

"Be quiet," a woman admonished. But the baby only cried louder. "Waa-aah! Waa-aah!"

"Shut up!" I yelled, and banged on the wall. But all night, the baby kept crying, preventing me from sleeping.

My parents checked us into the White House Hotel near

Great Portland Street for a few days until our flat was ready. Just as in Scotland, the English sky was low and filled with thick clouds. There was no sun, only sunny intervals, or so called by the TV weatherman. Everyone—black, white, Asian, and everything in between—plodded listlessly, as if they were living underwater. There seemed to be an air of depression over everything. Even the food, including at the Italian restaurant in the hotel, where every night the pasta was soggy and the sauce flat, the decor ugly, and the waiters unfriendly.

In the basement of the hotel, my brothers swam in the pool, submerged in their own world. I walked the streets by myself, trying to stave off a feeling of dissipation into a void. I glanced at myself as I passed long rows of shop windows, confirming that there was no one who looked even vaguely like me. Red double-decker buses and black taxis jammed the wide roads all the way to Piccadilly Circus and Oxford Street and a place named Leicester Square that I couldn't figure out how to pronounce. Each area was marked with a round red, blue, and white sign of the underground station. Oxford Street was packed with people and shopping bags that banged against my legs as I passed by. Near Bond Street, I saw a sign—Harley Street. I turned the opposite way so I didn't have to remember Dr. Fortuna and the book of noses.

As I walked I felt as invisible as when I had accidentally peed while waiting at a bus stop behind a queue of people in Glasgow shortly after we'd moved there. Even though it wasn't raining, for a change, and the yellow pee ran down the pavement in front of everyone, no one so much as glanced at me. It was as if I didn't exist, and I didn't know what felt worse, my shame at losing control or that no one noticed.

At the corner of Half Moon Street, I came upon a store selling Scottish tartans and Aran sweaters. A sign in gold lettering read "Duty Free for International Visitors." Was that me? Was I a visitor, or was I here for good?

Our new flat was so near the hotel, we could walk there. But my father made us get into a taxi—only one this time because Ava and Natalie were gone and Kirk and my mother were already at the flat, unpacking new furniture. My father, in a folding seat facing the back, ordered me to get in next to him. Tense and alert, he warned the driver to be careful how he loaded our suitcases. I refused to let anyone touch my guitar and carefully propped it against my knees.

"Where are we going, Dad?" asked Rock in a small voice. He was so tightly stuffed into the seat, you could have said "Boo" and watched him pop out of it like a balloon.

"I know where," nodded Marilyn importantly. She wore a new red dress with a black bow that my mother had bought on Oxford Street. "We're going to our new apartment."

"Flat," corrected Fig. "You have to say flat."

Marilyn stuck out her tongue at him. "Fla-aat, fla-aat. Think you know everything."

The taxi halted outside a five-story brick building with a revolving door at the entrance. An old man in a black uniform stood outside, tipping his hat when he saw my father. "Good day to you, sir," he said, and climbed down the steps to help the driver. As he carried up our cases two by two he winked at me. I glowered back.

The flat was on the third floor, except it was called the second, because in Britain, the first floor turned out to be the ground floor. Our door had three locks on it and faced the elevator shaft. The apartment was the shape of a horseshoe with two living rooms and four bedrooms. One of the living rooms, the one next to my parents' bedroom, had a wall of paneled glass separating it from the hallway. When he was home, it became my father's resting place and he sat with his back to the glass amid the pink and rosewood furniture, chain-smoking and pouring whisky from Johnnie Walker bottles. The other living room was for watching television. My mother tsked loudly and switched it off whenever there was any kissing on it.

"Mom, that was in the middle of the show!" protested Kirk.

"I don't care. I don't want you watching that filth." She put her feet on the matching stool and opened a magazine. Blinking rapidly, she sent one false eyelash off kilter so that it hung from the corner of her eye. I nudged Kirk, smirking. He looked at me blankly, then turned away.

My father opened his office on Whitehall, right near Trafalgar Square where a statue of Nelson stood high off the ground, covered in pigeon shit. The building was made of gray stone, also plastered in shit, dry little white ones. My father's office was on the fourth floor.

"I want you and Kirk to help me out," he said at breakfast. "That idiot secretary didn't turn up again."

"Better be careful what you say," said my mother. "They have lots of strikes here."

My father grimaced. "Not in my office." He put down his cup. "I'll pay you."

I didn't tell him it wasn't necessary. I was dying to see what he did.

The office had two rooms, glossy white walls, and mahogany doors. One of the doors had a glass panel on which was written, in thick gold lettering, A. R. Rung, Esq., President. I didn't know what the R. stood for. The walls were blank, as was my father's desk inside the room adjoining the one we entered, except for a black telephone and metal trays marked In, Out, and Pending. There were no photographs or wall hangings, or decorations of any kind, only a series of doors declaring Chairman of the Board, Chief Financial Officer, and Vice President. No one ever came in or out of those doors, and when I turned the handles, the doors didn't move. They were just doors, with no rooms behind.

Stacks of envelopes, letters, and brochures covered a large rectangular desk, which was to be our workplace. Our job was to stuff the letters and brochures into the envelopes and seal them with red wax that dripped from a stick. My father had an emblem on the seal, a lion with a mouse between its teeth. The company was called Lion, Ltd.

"But Dad, that's cruel," said Kirk, examining the seal. "Why did you do that?"

My father chuckled. "So they know who's boss."

I read the letters, but they didn't tell me anything about my father. They were all the same, saying that the company distilled whisky and how to invest in its increasing value. A brochure my father had printed showed images of six different types of whisky. None of them was the one my father was always drinking, Johnnie Walker.

"But what do you do, Dad?" I asked. This didn't seem like anything I had heard him and my mother talking about. When Mr. McKenzie had visited us at Dougalls Holiday Camp after our arrival in Scotland, he said something about whisky and marketing. But I had never seen or heard anything about it. What my father did seemed as mysterious as in every other place we'd lived. Money, fish, gambling, whisky—once my mother even said that he worked in insurance, when we lived in Miami Beach. Now, all of a sudden, he had an office, one that I could see with my own eyes.

My father looked distracted. "What does it look like? I sell whisky."

"Did you do that in Scotland?"

His brow darkened. "Why are you always asking questions? Just concentrate on your work. And stop spilling wax onto the letters."

The phone rang a few times, and I could hear my father picking it up from his desk. But the glass panel was too thick for me to make out what he was saying.

Kirk and I worked for a week, until the secretary came back. I earned five pounds and ten shillings and slipped it under my mattress.

stared in the mirror at my stomach. It was flat, but my period hadn't come for weeks.

"What should I do?" I whispered into the phone, shaking.

"Oh, my god," Natalie answered. Her voice was low, wary, and she seemed very far away. "Pee into a bottle and take it to the pharmacy. Tell them you'll come back to get the answer."

I stole into the bathroom and found an aspirin bottle. I flushed the pills down the toilet and tried to aim into the bottle. Some of the hot liquid poured onto my hands and I started crying, feeling dirty. Then I wrapped the bottle in a paper bag and hid it at the back of my closet. The next time my mother told me to pick up milk from the store, I went to the pharmacy and dropped the bottle off.

"Very well, then," said the pharmacist, taking it from me. "The results will be ready in a week."

Seven days later, when my period still hadn't come, I went back. The pharmacist's eyes narrowed. "Is this for you?" he frowned.

"No," I said quickly. "For my mother."

His face brightened. "Well, you can tell her the happy news. She's going to have a baby."

I leaned against the counter, feeling faint.

"What's the matter?" he asked, sounding concerned. "Are you all right?" His expression suddenly changed. "It's not hers, is it," he said coldly.

"Leave me alone," I stammered and ran out of the store to call Natalie while my parents were still out. "He's going to kill me!" I sobbed.

"Calm down," Natalie said tersely. "It'll be okay."

"No, it won't. He's going to kill me. What am I going to do?" I wailed.

"Who's going to kill you?" a voice boomed behind me. My father's hand ripped the phone from my hand. He hung it up and yanked me around to face him, still with his coat on. "What exactly am I going to kill you over?"

"Nothing, Dad," I cried.

He took my hair in his hands and twisted my head to the side. "Don't treat me like an idiot. I can pick up the phone and ask Natalie. You know she'll tell me so you might as well do it first."

"It's nothing, Dad."

He lifted the phone, glowering at me, and dialed.

"It's nothing," I said. "I swear."

"Natalie?" he said into the receiver.

"I'm pregnant," I blurted, ducking.

His eyes widened. "You're what?"

"I'm pregnant!" I burst into tears.

My father threw the receiver against the wall. "Get over here!" he shouted, thumping his fist in the air.

My mother appeared from the kitchen. "What's going on?"

My father pushed me into the living room surrounded by glass. "Sit down!"

My mother asked plaintively, "Will someone please tell me what's going on?"

My father's hands shook as he pulled out a cigarette. With a sound of fury, he mashed it between his fingers. "She's pregnant."

My mother gasped. "Pregnant?"

"Who was it?" my father said menacingly through clenched teeth.

My mother's eyes grew beady.

"His name's John," I began weakly.

"John," my father mocked with flashing eyes. "Who's he?"

I thought about the bathroom and the needle in John's arm. "I don't know. Just someone."

"Where did you meet him?" My father inhaled deeply after he lit a cigarette.

"In Glasgow."

"Where did you go?"

Sweat poured down the sides of my nose. "I don't know. To his house."

My father crushed out his cigarette. "Where was it?"

"Aaron," my mother interrupted. "Why do you need to know where it was? Don't upset yourself like this."

"Where?" shouted my father.

"I don't know! Near Byers Road."

"Byers Road, eh?" My father drew a deep breath. His voice sounded like gravel. "What were you doing on Byers Road?"

"I don't know." I wiped moisture from my upper lip.

"What day and time was it?"

"I don't know! Two weeks ago. Four o'clock?"

"Well, at least you didn't miss any school." He laughed angrily. "How pregnant are you?"

"I don't know!"

"When was your last period?"

I lifted my head, shocked. I didn't know he knew about periods. "Um . . . around the last week of April," I stuttered.

"Around the last week of April. That means you should have had"—he counted on his fingers—"two periods by now." A muscle quivered in the pouch beneath his eye. "So that means you must be more than two months pregnant." He sprang up and slapped me hard on the head. "You slut! Whore! How many other men have you slept with?"

My mother's lip curled. "How do you think the other kids are going to feel, knowing their fourteen-year-old sister is pregnant?" she hissed. "What kind of influence do you call yourself?"

"Stop it!" I shielded my face with my hands and didn't see

my father's fist aimed at my abdomen. When it landed, I doubled over, choking.

My mother's voice floated above me. "Don't," she said to my father. "You'll have a heart attack." She pinched my chin hard, pulling my face up so that I looked into her pinpoint eyes. "Look at what you're doing!"

"It's not my fault!"

My father grabbed me as I tried to escape from her grip, and threw me against the wall.

"Oh no you don't, young lady. You get back in here. You're not finished yet."

My mother folded her arms. "She's got to have an abortion."

"But I don't want an abortion."

"She doesn't want an abortion." My mother's voice was sarcastic, scathing.

"So she's planning to have this baby?" snorted my father. "And who does she think is going to look after it?"

"She thinks she's old enough to have a baby. She's only fourteen, but she knows how to feed it, to change diapers, to put up with all the noise, the ingratitude, to do all the dirty work." My mother's resentment oozed from each word.

My father spat out, "And how does she think she's going to support it? Where's the money going to come from?"

"Maybe she thinks her boyfriend, is that what she called him, Mr. Byers Road, has money for her and the baby."

My father lit a cigarette. "She thinks money grows on trees.

Of course, she's never had to support herself a day in her life, but that's okay, she knows how to support herself and a baby."

"But I don't want an abortion!" I yelled.

My father eyes bulged. "You shut up! Don't say another word."

"You can't make me," I whimpered.

Towering over me, my father slowly unbuckled his belt. Winding it around his hand, he threatened, "Don't you dare say another word!"

"You can't make me!" I shrieked.

Snap! The leather stung my arms and legs as he whipped me. "This is my house!" he yelled. "You have to do what I say! You bitch! You fuck! You cunt!"

I convulsed in a shock wave from hearing my father swear. Suddenly, I grew still. I watched the vein in his forehead turn blue and knotted. As he swung the belt over and over again I silently relished his loss of control, filled with satisfaction that I could overpower him by doing nothing at all. My mother stood by the door, observing me in horror.

The next morning, stiff and sore, I threw up. "Mom, I'm sick," I moaned, going into the kitchen.

She turned away with a look of repulsion. "You should be grateful something can be done. It's illegal, you know. You don't know how lucky you are." She spun back around. "And if you dare mention one word of this to the rest of the family, you are in deep trouble. Don't you dare."

"Don't dare what, Mom?" Fig asked as he appeared rubbing sleep from his eyes.

"None of your business. And tell your brothers and sister to keep away from Tosca. None of you are to come near her or speak to her. Do you hear me?"

Fig glanced quickly at me and ran out of the room.

started throwing up in the morning. "Mom, I feel sick," I whined in the local grocery store where I had to accompany her to buy food.

"Shh," she said, her eyes darting furtively over her shoulder as we walked back home up Marylebone Lane. "You should be grateful something can be done. It's against the law; you could get us all into trouble. You don't know how lucky you are."

Her eyes tightened. She'd stopped bothering to take off her makeup at night, merely reapplying more of it the next day, and thick turquoise arches caked her upper eyelids. "Come with me," she commanded, grabbing my arm.

"Stop it, Mom," I cried, trying to pull away.

My mother yanked open the door to Marie's Hair Salon and pushed me inside. "I want an appointment right now," she said as if the receptionist was planning on giving her a hard time. But no other customers were in the shop, only two hairdressers sitting at the back smoking cigarettes in their blue nylon coats.

"Mom," I screeched.

"I want it all off," she ordered the hairdresser who had risen to her feet and wouldn't meet my eyes even after she stubbed out her cigarette. The hairdresser tied a light blue gown around me and directed me to the sink with a black hose wrapped around the faucets. I felt bile rise in my throat and swallowed hard.

"I'm going to be sick," I moaned.

My mother raised her hand. "Just you dare."

I forced it back as the hairdresser pulled my head back into the sink. My mother stood by with her arms folded, glaring furiously. I cried silently in front of the mirror as the hairdresser worked her way around my head, starting at the back and following my mother's directions to shear it all off. Each long clump of hair that fell on the floor felt like a slap across the head. Every lost strand uncovered more of my ugliness, until my face stood out in the world completely exposed, big, ugly, and littered with freckly blotches. No one would want me now.

"All right, then," said the hairdresser. She stood back with her comb up, checking her work. There was nothing left, only little brown tufts that were so short they didn't touch my neck or brow.

"How much?" my mother asked, digging out her new sealskin purse.

The receptionist smiled politely as she handed over my mother's change, then held the door open.

I didn't look back to see whether the hairdresser who'd worked on me was relieved I was gone. The whole shop probably thought we were just a couple of crazy Americans.

———

Two weeks' confinement to my room, and finally the day came. My mother pushed me into a cab and threw in an overnight bag. She climbed in and pulled the door.

"Eltham Hospital," she said to the driver. The streets were streaked with moisture, but it had stopped raining. "And make it snappy." She pulled out her compact to apply another layer of lipstick.

I felt dead inside as the cab drove down Regent Street and then Whitehall, past my father's office with all those fake rooms, and over the Thames to the southern part of the city. The houses looked small and dank as we passed by one underground station after another. Finally, we turned into a wide road with gray houses on either side and pulled up to a three-story hospital.

"Don't think it was easy," my mother reminded me at the entrance. "No one's allowed to have one, let alone a fourteen-year-old."

I jerked out of her grip. "Gee, Mom, thanks."

"Shut up," she hissed.

The head nurse sat behind a desk up a flight of stairs. Labour Ward, read the sign above the entrance.

"Yes, come this way," she said, leading us along the dull beige linoleum floors and pale green walls to a private room. Farther along the corridor lay rows of beds surrounded by screens. The sound of babies crying and women laughing and chatting rose above them.

"We put her in a room of her own. Better not to say anything, we don't want any trouble," said the nurse curtly. She nodded to me. "Get undressed. You have to be weighed."

I skulked behind the closet door and changed into the hospital gown she held with the tips of her fingers.

"Poor thing," she said to my mother. "I don't know how you cope."

My mother ignored her. "Come out of there," she said to me. She tapped her foot as I was weighed and measured and my blood pressure taken. Another nurse came in carrying a bowl of water and a razor and instructed me to lie on the sheet. She placed a towel underneath, then, with deft strokes, shaved my vagina as I sobbed.

My mother tsked. "Stop crying!" She stood up stiffly and clutched her handbag. "You do what they say."

After she strode out, loudly clicking her heels, I said to the nurse, "I don't want to do it, you know. They're making me. It's not fair."

She folded the towel and picked up the bowl. "I wouldn't know anything about that."

On strict orders to stay in my room, I drew aside the curtains to look outside. But the window only faced a wall of mottled gray stone. I slowly opened the door and crept into the corridor.

"Where do you think you're going?" A nurse caught me from around the corner.

Scared, I slipped back into my room and lit a cigarette, dragging hard before blasting smoke out of the window.

At the crack of dawn, a portly man in a white coat entered my room and told me to turn over. "Take a deep breath," he said, jabbing me hard.

"Ow!" I yelped. He ignored me and said someone would come and get me in a few minutes.

I felt drowsy and tried to fight it, but soon felt myself sliding downward. I awoke briefly when I was lifted back into bed in my hospital room. When I came to, my mouth felt like it was filled with gauze and my stomach hurt. I squeezed the buzzer, and then again when no one came. A nurse finally appeared, clucking.

"I'm thirsty," I said thickly.

"Oh you are, are you?" she reprimanded. "There's a glass on the table. Don't you know we have more important things to do?"

"Slag," she muttered under her breath as she whished out.

After wetting my throat, I fell back to sleep, and when I awoke again, a crack in the curtain showed night had fallen. The only feeling I had was hunger. I squeezed the buzzer six times before someone came.

"What do you think this is, a hotel?" said the nurse when I asked for food. "I'll bring you a piece of bread."

It was a piece of bread, nothing else. I felt as they wanted me to—ugly, sinful, and dirtier than the dirtiest piece of dirt.

When I got home, my drawers were empty, my clothes gone. My father shook his fist.

"You tell anyone about where you were and you're in for it.

Come with me." He walked me along the hallway and pointed to the moldings close to the floor. "Get a bucket and a cloth and wash every molding in the house."

"The days of you doing whatever you want are over." My mother stood close to me, pointing her finger in my face.

My father continued. "You're not allowed to go out except to school. Kirk will escort you. You are to help your mother in the kitchen—dishes after every meal."

While I was on my hands and knees, my mother stood over me. "I never had sex before I was married," she sniffed, straightening her blouse with sanctimony.

"Bully for you," I hissed.

"What?" she said, stiffening.

"Nothing," I mumbled, scrubbing away.

Two weeks after my abortion, my father announced we were going on vacation. "That's what we need, Luce. A real vacation."

I couldn't care less if we were moving or not. What difference would it make?

The days in the Channel Islands passed in a haze of forcing down three meals a day in the hotel restaurant and following my mother while she shopped. With my plain A-line polyester skirt, sensible walking shoes, and a ten-month-old nose, I hardly recognized myself. But I still had my guitar, the guitar Natalie had painted for me. It was only during the day, when I sat in the hotel room I shared with Marilyn with the curtains drawn, playing "Greensleeves" over and over again, that I felt any kind of stirring inside, that this was my body and I was still in it. At night, I put the guitar at the foot of my bed so it was the last thing I saw at night and the first thing in the morning.

On the day of our departure, my guitar was not at the foot of my bed. I sprang up and circled the room, searching under our beds, the bathroom, and the closet.

"What's wrong, Tosca?" Marilyn asked with a worried expression on her face.

"Where is it?" I shrieked. "Who took it?"

I belted into my brothers' room, but it wasn't there either. Fig glanced up from his book.

"What's the matter?" he said. "You look funny."

I raced along to my parents' room. Fast asleep, they were stretched out in the double bed, smaller than the combination of the twin beds they always slept in at home, with the blankets smoothly covering the bumps and angles of their bodies. As they spooned, my mother faced the door with her hand grasping my father's over her shoulder. Her face looked smooth and relaxed, and a slight smile grazed her lips. I was shocked. I had never seen her, or my father, like this, so content and peaceful.

"Mom! Dad! Wake up! There's been a robbery."

My mother shot up, her nightgown slipping off her shoulder, revealing newly sun-flushed skin. "What?" Her eyes came into focus. She scowled when she saw me. "What's going on?"

"Somebody stole my guitar! When I woke up it wasn't there!"

Blinking sleepily, my father reached for his bathrobe. "Go back to your room and get ready to leave," he commanded.

"Call the police!" I cried.

"Okay," he answered agreeably. "Get the other kids and wait for us in the lobby."

"Call them now!" I insisted. I stamped my foot. "I'm not leaving until they find my guitar."

"I said I would call them," he said, turning his back to me as he headed for the bathroom. "Now go back to your room and get ready."

In the lobby, I ran up to my father at the front desk where he was settling the bill. "What did the police say?"

"I'll call them at the airport." His face was freshly shaved, round, waxy, his eyes clear blue and crinkled in the corners.

"I'm not leaving until it's found," I repeated, panicked.

"Get into the cab." He pushed me. "I said I'd call them at the airport."

"Dad, call the police!" I cried again at the airport after we checked in.

"Oh for Christ's sake, I'll go and call them now," he said angrily and stalked off to the back of the airport. He came back a few minutes later, puffing on a cigarette. "They're looking into it. They'll call us in London when they find it."

The police never called and my guitar never turned up. On the way to school a few weeks later, Kirk said, "I saw Dad in the elevator the night before your guitar disappeared. He told me you were going to have a big shock when you woke up."

He looked away and shrugged when I cried, "Why didn't you stop him?"

Back in London, I lay on my bed. The room was soundless, the air still. "If there's a God," I said, clasping my hands, "show me a sign." I stared intently at the ceiling. "I'll give you to the count of ten." Ten turned into twenty-five, twenty-five turned into one hundred. Outside, the rain fell down in sheets, tap-tapping against the window. I rolled over and stared at a row of black taxis lined up at the traffic lights like a funeral procession. I curled my fist. I was going to let the bastard have it.

After breakfast, lunch, and supper, I did the dishes as I had to. But in my mind, I pictured my parents' faces on the plates and hurled them into the sink. I rattled the spoons and forks as loudly as I could and crashed the glasses into the draining board. I burned so many holes in my father's shirts that my mother stopped me from ironing, and when both of them were out, I snuck into their bathroom where my father's socks were drying on a clotheshorse. I filled the sink with water and soaped each sock, one by one, diligently rubbing the soles where my father's feet were most allergic, brimming with glee as he hopped in the kitchen at breakfast, complaining that his feet were on fire. I dumped whisky from his bottles, just enough so he wouldn't know, and filled them to the top again with water. But my greatest victory was stealing his gold cigarette case, the one he had carried in his pocket from New York, through Mexico, Nassau, Florida, Scotland, and now England, the one he tapped his cigarette against while I sat before him quaking. I tossed it out the back window of the subway car on the way to school. He had foolishly left the case on the rosewood table in the living room while he slept. With grim satisfaction, I counted the bounces against the tracks as we sped out of the tunnel, almost hearing the sound of guitar strings resounding against the whooshing and flailing of the train.

My parents decided to send us to a private school, one that covered all ages. "It's more convenient," they said. The admission process required an IQ test, and a series of appointments were made. On a Wednesday at three o'clock, I traveled to St. John's Wood with my mother. Her face was a rainbow of color, and tiny specks of gold and silver flashed on her cheeks— the lipstick, the eye shadow, the false eyelashes, and now glitter. I scrubbed my face raw so I would look nothing like her.

I answered questions, drew pictures, and filled in a quiz, which was then reviewed by a psychoanalyst, who met with my mother in a private room to discuss the results.

"Your IQ is one hundred and thirty-five," said my mother on the way home. "That must be why you keep getting into trouble. Just like your father."

I looked at her for more information, but that was it. Zip.

The following Monday, I had to wait for the others to get ready as my father wouldn't let me go to school on my own. Two adjoining houses made up the school in Hampstead, an area where famous people were supposed to live. My mother was thrilled.

"All those famous actors are there," she said, excitedly.

"Which ones, Mom?" asked Rock.

"What does it matter?" she said, irritated. "Famous ones."

There was no one famous at the school. Except for me, who achieved the status by being suspended the first week. I was knitting in the break and still knitting when Mrs. Newsome, my English teacher, raised her chalk to start the class.

"Put your knitting away," she said, looking reproachfully at me over her reading glasses.

"Okay," I said calmly. I kept knitting.

She rapped her ruler on the podium. "Now!"

"Okay, when I finish this row."

The veins on her temples popped out. "Tosca Rung, you do as I say!"

I threw down the wool and knocked back my chair. "Fuck off!"

There was a shocked silence. Her mouth opened and closed like a fish. "You get down to the headmistress right now!"

The headmistress's skin was lightly freckled, and her hair swung across her brow as she moved, reflecting red glints from the sun that poured into her office.

"Why don't you sit down?" She smiled, gesturing to a soft chair by her desk. "Your teacher tells me you're not very happy," she said, raising her eyebrows gently. Her eyes were a soft gray, the same shade as her sweater.

I shrugged.

"Tosca, it is Tosca, isn't it? What do you want to be? What do you want to do with your life?" she asked.

Her hands played with an eraser on her glossy walnut desk.

"I don't know," I mumbled. "Be a teacher, I guess." I stared at her, defiantly. "I'd treat the kids really well."

She laughed. "I'm sure you would make a wonderful teacher."

"Really," I answered belligerently. I didn't want her to be so nice.

"Yes, if you just put your mind to it. Stay home for the rest of the day, then come back tomorrow, ready to make friends. I'll talk to your teacher."

I glared down the hallway when she let me out. Fat chance I would become a teacher. Anyway, I reasoned, striking a match against the banister to light a cigarette, she has to be nice to me. The school was private and they must have needed the money.

My father was out of town and my mother in the hospital again so they didn't find out about my suspension, especially because I got back to the school gates in time to go home with the others, scared they'd tell on me. When my father came back, he and Kirk stayed up late talking in the kitchen.

"Everyone has to be nice to Mom when she returns," said my father. "It's her nerves."

"Yeah," said Kirk. I could imagine him swelling with importance at my father's confidence in him.

My father changed the subject. "Things are going well in

my office. Maybe you'd like to come and work for me one day."

"I don't know, Dad." There was a tremor in Kirk's voice. "My teacher said I should be a decorator. He said I have a good eye for detail."

My father laughed. "You don't want to be a decorator. That's for pansies."

"Why do you always use that word, Dad?" Kirk retorted angrily. His chair grated against the floor. "It's not fair! Leave me alone!"

He ran out the front door. Stunned, my father chased out after him.

"Come back!" he called down the corridor. "You can't go out. It's late!" A few moments later, there was the sound of two bodies struggling and they came back, my father tugging Kirk by his collar.

"Whoever said you were a pansy?"

From the doorway, I saw Kirk blush and move his lips, stuttering silently. Then he ran to his room. My father remained there, shaking his head in confusion.

At school, I made friends as the headmistress suggested. Toby, my classmate, exchanged joints for the pills I stole from my mother's medicine cabinet. My mother had all kinds of pills now, amphetamines, tranquilizers, and sleeping pills.

Clear-eyed and unafraid, Toby liked them all. He sat next to me and scribbled notes, laughing at the teachers and making up poems. His mother had left him with his father, who was hardly ever home, when he was two.

"I don't give a shit," he wrote. "Stuff him."

I wrote back, "I wouldn't give a shit either."

In the breaks, I took the joints to the small bathroom at the top of the stairs and smoked them out the window.

The week of Christmas, the ground was covered in a light snow. I hadn't been out since last Friday, except to go shopping with my mother, and school wasn't to start for another week. I picked the scab off my arm where I had scratched myself in one long line. I felt like I was suffocating. I ran into Kirk's room.

"Kirk, please," I begged. "Can we go out?"

He looked up from his book. "I don't feel like going out," he said. "I'm busy."

"Please. Dad won't let me go out alone, and you're the only one I can ask."

"Leave me alone. It's too cold. I don't want to go."

"What if Toby comes?" I blurted, remembering the way at recess Toby was always staring at Kirk and how Kirk looked back through half-closed eyes, smiling sleepily. He never acted like that at home.

Kirk gave a start. "Do you think he will?"

I nodded, trying to suppress my eagerness. "Here's his number. Call him."

My brother blushed. "No, you do it. Go on."

"Yes, that would be super," said Toby on the phone. "Maybe we can go for tea or to my house or something."

"Great," I said. "What time can we meet?"

"How about in an hour?"

"Be back at five," said my mother, looking up from her magazine. "I'm not sure I should let you out at all."

I pulled Kirk's arm. "Come on. Before she changes her mind." I fidgeted impatiently as he tied his new suede Hush Puppies in the hallway. "Come on, hurry up," I hissed.

"Piss off," he said, not looking up.

Toby was already waiting at Marble Arch tube where he said he would be, at the top of the steps. He was dressed in a dark blue maxi trench coat. His hair was sopping wet, and he shivered in the wind blowing over from Hyde Park. Rain pounded the street in torrents, splashing down the concrete stairs. But I could have been in the middle of an Arctic blizzard for all I cared as I ran exuberantly up the steps.

A woman in red high heels careened down the street, pouring into the station and shaking the wet out of her hair as she went, swearing under her breath. I slipped to the side to let her pass as I greeted Toby cheerfully.

"Hiya," he responded, casting a glance over at Kirk, who avoided eye contact. Toby glanced back at me quizzically.

I shoved my hands in my pockets as I peered out at the rain. "What do you fancy doing?"

"I can't stay long," said Toby nonchalantly. "The old man said I have to be there when his new girlfriend comes over."

"Fuck," I said dejectedly. "Can we come over to your house?"

"Sorry," Toby said, slouching into his coat. He'd just come back from a rare visit with his mother who had moved to Spain. He'd missed school for a week and came back tan and miserable. His nose was still peeling, and he didn't look as confident as he had when he loped through the yard at school.

"How about going to the Wimpy?" he mumbled.

We ran down a few doors into a dreary diner decked with plastic-covered tables that cast a sickly hue beneath greasy chips and faux hamburgers, poetically named beefburgers on the ketchup-spattered menu. Kirk looked strangely discomfited and kept his head down eating, licking a smear of ketchup off the side of his palm. Toby wolfed down his burger not saying much either, then wiped his long fingers on a thin coarse inch of napkin and lit a cigarette, blowing smoke sophisticatedly out of the side of his mouth. He contemplated the air with blood-shot eyes, an abashed half-smile on his face. I didn't know what to say. I'd never seen Toby outside school, and he seemed so distant, so preoccupied, so unsure of himself. We paid, handing over the money to a pint-size waitress, then poured back out to the street through the glass door, which was, surprisingly, splashed in watery sunlight, the sky no longer pelting with rain.

"Thank fuck," I said with false heartiness, cocking my head

across the way toward Hyde Park, clutching at straws to stay out as long as I could. "Want to go for a walk?"

Toby shook his head uncomfortably, balancing on the sides of his shoes. "Sorry, I can't." He gave a perfunctory wave and slouched off into Edgware Road.

I looked after him, dispirited. "Let's go for a walk."

Kirk gazed after Toby with a look of disgust on his face. "He's so boring. What do you talk about? He doesn't say anything."

I prickled defensively. "You didn't either."

I felt guilty at Kirk's hurt expression. "Why do you always have to be so mean?" he scowled, turning away from me.

"Come on," I said cajolingly. "Let's go get a bottle of wine. I've got some money."

"Wine?" He cocked an eyebrow, giggling.

"Yeah, come on, it'll be great. We can go down to Piccadilly Circus and hang around there."

"But what if Mom and Dad find out?"

I tutted. "They won't know. I've done it tons of times. Come on, Kirk, you'll love it. I'll show you where I used to go before," my voice trailed off, "you know," I finished lamely.

He shrugged. "Okay, it's all the same to me."

I sauntered along next to him, buoyant, thinking Kirk wasn't such a goody-goody after all. I walked slowly to keep in with his stride, hoping people would know I was his sister because, to my shock, he suddenly seemed so good looking. His hair had grown over his ears and neck in thick black curls, and now that he was older, his face looked more even, his nose straight and his lips full.

"Thanks for going out with me," I said clumsily.

Kirk shrugged again. "That's all right," he said awkwardly.

On the way to Piccadilly Circus, he waited outside while I nipped into an off license to buy a bottle of VP wine with the last of the money I'd saved from my week of working for my father. We sat on the steps leading up to the statue of Eros drinking from a paper bag, surrounded by traffic and a smattering of hippies lying about on the damp concrete. I breathed in the car fumes, ecstatic to be out in the city. While Kirk and I passed the bottle back and forth, I told him about walking around when we'd first moved, and how men used to whistle at me and think I was a prostitute.

"It's different for girls," Kirk slurred, burping over the paper bag. "No one even notices me."

"You're lucky," I harrumphed. I looked around. A skinny, long-faced man in a brown leather jacket and hair straggling down his shoulders vaulted over the railings at the edge of the circle. I squinted drunkenly at him. He seemed familiar. He looked up as he approached Eros and then I realized it was McCrystal, who used to go to the Red Lion in Glasgow and had a crush on Ava.

He recognized me at the same time. "Tosca!" His lips parted in a huge grin, making him look toothy and happy in spite of his long hangdog face. His thin cheeks cleaved with dimples. "Wha' are yew doin' here?"

Kirk glanced at him sleepily. "Who'sh that?"

"A friend of Ava's," I said, making room for McCrystal to sit down next to us, feeling a twinge of nostalgia at his accent. "Do you want some wine?" I asked, offering him the paper bag.

"Aye, thanks," he said, slugging from the bottle, his eyelids drooping low over his thick curly lashes behind his glasses. He wiped his chin and gave the bottle back. He grinned at me. "Fancy going for a smoke?" he said.

"All right," I said, weaving to my feet. "Kirk, wait here until I come back. I'm going for a walk. I'll be back in a few minutes."

"Okay," he said, examining his new Hush Puppies now stained with rain.

"Wait for me," I ordered him sternly. Turning to McCrystal, I said, "All right, then, let's go," and half-ran beside his long strides as we headed down Haymarket. The shops and galleries were closed and the pavement was gray and stark with the holiday emptiness in spite of the cars racing down the broad road, their taillights burning brightly.

"What are you doing in London?" I asked.

"I've got to get a job," he said. "I'm desperate."

"What do you do?" I asked curiously.

"Anything." McCrystal's wire-rimmed glasses reflected the pale orange light of the streetlights. He looked at me closely. "Why did you cut off all your hair? It was beautiful."

I flushed at the unexpected compliment, my eyes stinging as I passed the joint back to him. We huddled side by side against a brick wall in the narrow alley.

"My parents made me," I said finally. "I got pregnant."

"God," said McCrystal his eyes widening as the butt of the joint glowed and died again. "I didn't know you were old enough."

"Yes, I am," I said defensively.

"Sorry, hen," he said morosely, "I didn't mean to embarrass you." He took another drag, then passed me back the joint, gazing at me pensively. "Do you fancy going for a drink?"

"What time is it?" I said, suddenly remembering Kirk.

McCrystal pushed up his sleeve. "Seven-thirty."

"Shit," I cried. "I was supposed to be home at five. I'm going to get killed!" I started running. "I've got to go." I dashed for Haymarket and back up to Piccadilly Circus.

"Mind how you go!" McCrystal yelled from behind.

I hurtled over the railings around the statue, the metal stinging icily under my bare fingers. Kirk was nowhere to be seen. I raced the whole way home.

My father opened the front door with a petrifying look on his face.

"Dad," I panted out of breath, praying Kirk hadn't said anything.

He gripped my ear and wrested me into the window living room. Perched on the couch sat Kirk, his head bowed. My mother's face twisted in anger.

"You should be ashamed of yourself, getting your brother drunk and leaving him in the street."

"Where did you go?" my father growled.

"I was just walking around." I licked my dry lips. "Honest."

"I said you weren't allowed to be out without someone in the family! I said you weren't to be out of your brother's sight for one second! You disobeyed me! Where did you go?"

"Nowhere, I just went to buy something and when I got back Kirk had gone. I told him to wait, I wasn't doing anything."

"If I find out—"

"He came home and threw up over everything," my mother interrupted angrily. "I trusted you, and look what you did!"

I started crying. "I didn't do anything! I told him to wait! It's not my fault he left!"

"Come on, Kirk," my mother said stiffly, her chin in the air, tapping him on the shoulder. "You have to go to bed. You'll feel better in the morning." She didn't mention how much experience she must have had with that, with my father. Kirk rolled to his feet. His face was completely white.

After my mother closed the window door behind them, my father sat motionlessly, his eyes rock hard, flat blue. I cupped my head in my palm to stop it from shaking.

My father's broad chest was hidden beneath his shirt and a sky blue cashmere cardigan that made his shirt look even whiter. The neck was open, the button undone after he'd unstrung the tie that lay casually across the flat planes of his chest. A few stray hairs rose above the button, thick black hairs reaching up to the base of his Adam's apple, which swung dangerously in his neck.

I ducked.

My father slowly removed his hands from the armrests, smoothed down his sleeves, and stood up. The thick bulbs of his fingertips loomed closer. He placed his hands, firm and smooth, on my neck. I felt myself rising in the air as he lifted me off the couch.

"Dad!" I choked.

"When are you going to stop?" he yelled.

"Get off me!" I bellowed as I struggled to free myself. My hand curled into a fist and swung effortlessly through the air. My father's dense shoulder met my hand with full force. The shock of the impact ricocheted up my arm, making me reel back.

"I hate you, you fucking bastard!" I shouted.

"Why, you little bitch!" He slapped me so hard my head snapped back. I bobbed on my feet, listing from side to side until I got my balance back, then with a strangled yelp I flew at him with raised fists. I pummeled the broad planes of his chest, the curves of his upper arms and stomach, which sickeningly lurched, making him grunt way high above me. He wrapped tufts of my hair between his fingers and pulled down so hard I crashed to the floor. I kicked and punched whatever parts of him I could reach, his skinny calves with the little black hairs, his garters stabbing into my knuckles, making them wet with blood, pedaling hard into his thighs and knees, screaming and heaving in air and his sweat. He punched and kicked me back with all his might, his toe jabbing me in the ribs over and over again. I shook with the impact, the nauseating sound·of my flesh and his blood thudding in my ears as I clawed at him, cutting into the cells of his body. I thrilled with satisfaction at his cries way above me. Suddenly, he got me by the loops of my pants. The skin at my waist caught in the grooves of the carpet, the burn searing into my flesh as he dragged me to my feet. He held me by the neck with his hands, then tightened them and squeezed hard. "You little bitch!" he grunted.

Suddenly I grew cold as ice. "Yes, that's what I am. A little bitch."

His eyes bulged as he clasped my neck tighter.

"That's right," I choked, my voice rasping at the back of my throat. "Kill me, you bastard."

We stood staring at each other in hatred. Then he shuddered and flung his hands down, seeming to realize what he was do-ing. "If you want to live here, you have to obey me," he panted.

I doubled over in a fit of coughing. "Okay, I'll leave," I croaked.

"Go to your room," he stammered. "Think about it." He paused. "I'll wait for your answer in my room."

I stuffed my three LPs, two shirts, and a pair of pants into a bag and strode into my parents' room. My mother lay with her feet splayed, reading *Woman's Own*. The bed was covered in a pale pink velour bedspread to match the curtains and the rose-colored carpet. My father perched on a pink velour stool at her vanity table, smoking a cigarette. I stopped just inside the doorway, squinting at them in disbelief. It looked like they had already forgotten about me.

"What do you want?" my father asked tersely. With satisfaction, I noticed three ragged welts on his hand where I'd scratched him.

"I'm leaving," I declared huskily, my throat raw from screaming. I could barely keep the jubilation from my voice.

"What?" my mother blurted, scandalized. "You can't leave. You're only fourteen."

"Watch me," I said, and turned on my heel.

My father stomped behind me to the front door. "Give me your key!"

"Here," I said, and holding my hand high, I dropped it on the floor with a loud ring. With a flourish, I yanked open the door and slammed it behind me with such a deafening crash it would be heard all the way to Australia. I was getting away from them forever. I was never coming back.

I floated elatedly all the way back to Piccadilly Circus. The steps around Eros were still littered with hippies. McCrystal sat on a middle step, smoking a roll-up as he gazed into space.

"Hello again, stranger," he greeted me with a smile. "What are you doing back here?"

"I left home," I boasted. "I'm going to hitchhike to Glasgow to stay with Natalie."

McCrystal passed me his tobacco pouch. "You're not going to hitchhike on your own, hen. It's too dangerous."

I scoffed. "I'll manage."

"Don't be stupid," he said. "Here, take this." He fished in his pocket and handed me ten pounds. "Get the coach." He patted me on the back. "Och, don't keep saying thanks, it's nae bother. Just go straight to the tube down to Victoria Station. I think there's a coach around ten or eleven. You'd better hurry."

A spray of moisture arced over the steps from a passing truck. "Get a job, you fucking layabouts!" the driver shouted.

"Fuck off!" a man behind us bellowed, making the woman next to him add, "Wanker!"

I hugged McCrystal and ran for the tube.

The ticket hall at the coach station was drafty and damp. The last coach of the day was listed at ten-thirty, arriving in Glasgow at six-thirty the next morning.

"Glasgow," I called impatiently through the slitted window, anxious I'd miss the coach, which was leaving in ten minutes.

"Single or return?" The ticket seller tiredly scratched his head beneath his cap.

"Single," I said with a thrill.

The bus was only half full and smelled of wet sweaters. I took a window seat near the back. The idling of the engine made something rattle in the overhead compartment. I breathed lightly to stop the twinges of pain in my ribs where my father had kicked me and placed my bag on the adjoining seat. The driver adjusted his rearview mirror one last time, and the coach began to move. The hot breath of the hydraulic brakes wheezed in through the windows as we staggered into Buckingham

Palace Road. I squashed down into my seat with my eyes level with the ashtray nailed into the seat in front. I was frightened that the bus might pass my father as we wound north through the streets of London, that he'd see me and force the bus to stop and make me get off. Only when we reached the country did I feel safe, with fields so dark in the moonless sky that nothing could be seen. I relaxed into the seat, nursing my swollen hand and gazing ahead through half-closed eyes, excited about seeing Natalie.

The bus stopped only once along the way, somewhere near Gretna Green. Half-asleep, I tottered off the bus behind the other passengers to a café serving strong, milky tea in thick-lipped china cups, the liquid so brown it looked like coffee. I bought a bar of Galaxy chocolate at the counter and nibbled it on my way back to the bus, luxuriating in being able to eat whatever I wanted.

The outskirts of Glasgow were layered in darkness, with only the occasional yellow light illuminating a window. Soon, graffiti-covered high-rises appeared in silhouette in the fog-laden dawn. Every so often a car zoomed past, the rays of its headlights briefly suspended over the odd playing field here and there, its grass glistening with frost. As we entered the city proper I felt a stab of nostalgia mixed with depression at the soot-stained buildings. I stumbled off the bus at the station, coughing in the billowing exhaust of coaches lumbering into the station, one on the tail of the other.

Natalie opened her door dressed in a bathrobe, rubbing sleep from her eyes. I took a step back, startled. Her short, straight hair fell over her thin face in a bob, and she was clad in a plain flannel nightgown beneath the pink polyester bathrobe. She looked so straight, nothing like the long-haired army-clothed hippie she used to be. More like a Scottish housewife.

She blinked in confusion, then exclaimed, "Tosca! You look so different. I hardly recognized you." She ushered me in and motioned with a finger to her lips. "Keep it down. Kevin's asleep."

I patted my short tufts of hair self-consciously and followed her down the hallway past her bedroom, stiffening at the sight of Kevin spread-eagled under the duvet before Natalie pulled the bedroom door to a quiet close. The next room down had a shiny wooden floor, on which sat an angular white couch with chrome armrests and legs at a right angle to a wall of stereo equipment, a tuner, and huge black speakers. A small brown cat climbed up the stack of shelves, mewing contentedly.

"I didn't know you had a cat," I said, a lump forming in my throat at the coziness, the homey-ness of it all, courtesy of my father's wedding gift of a down payment.

Natalie smiled and stroked the cat's fur with a soft look on her face. "Isn't she sweet?" she said.

"Lovely," I answered faintly.

In front of the couch was a matching glass and chrome coffee table. A neat pile of magazines rested at the corner of the table: *Architectural Design*, the cover read.

"Kevin's going to be an architect," Natalie said, catching my glance.

I felt a rush of jealousy at her solicitous expression as she led me into the sparkling white-walled kitchen across the hall with a small pine table positioned dead center.

"I can't believe I'm here," I exclaimed as I sat on a pine stool.

Natalie moved stiffly as she picked up a shiny new-looking electric kettle and readjusted a dishwashing sponge so that it rested at a perfect angle to the sink.

"What are you going to do?" she asked.

"Can I stay here?" I answered uncertainly.

Kevin's face appeared around the door, his expression surprisingly friendly. "Hullo, pip-squeak," he said, yawning in his blue terry-cloth bathrobe. "What happened to your hair?"

"Nothing," I mumbled, annoyed.

"Do you want an omelette? I'm making one for Kevin," Natalie said as she began cracking eggs on the side of a porcelain bowl.

I nodded sullenly. "Only if it's no trouble," I said resentfully.

"What are your plans?" Kevin said, biting a piece of toast.

Natalie poured the eggy mixture into a frying pan, then took off her glasses and rubbed them on her bathrobe, blinking myopically before putting them on again.

"So what have you been up to?" said Kevin, clearing his throat and stroking his chin. "How's life been treating you down in—"

Before he could finish the phone rang in the next room. Natalie looked nervous as Kevin jumped off the stool to answer it. She flipped the eggs, the muscle in her jaw pulsing. I held my breath, straining to hear.

"Natalie," I said beseechingly. "I can stay here, can't I?"

A faint tremor coursed down Natalie's back. The only sound was the crackling of grease in the frying pan. After a long pause, she turned with the spatula in her hand.

"Tosca," she started.

Kevin swung open the door, glancing at Natalie, then back at me. "It's your father."

"Say I'm not here," I warbled.

Kevin raised his hands, palms upward. "He said if you don't go back you're all going to get deported."

"You'd better go back," Natalie breathed, looking scared.

"Fuck him," I said angrily. "I don't give a shit."

Kevin continued. "He said if the police find out you're only fourteen and not living at home, they'll send the whole family out of the country."

"Do you think it's true?" Natalie asked him, moistening her lips.

Kevin shrugged. "Probably."

I scraped back my stool. "I'm not going back!" I searched Natalie's face for support.

Natalie twisted her hands. "You have to. You can't jeopardize the whole family like that."

"I can't go back!" I pleaded. "Please let me stay with you. Please!"

Natalie had a ragged look on her face. Even though she was only seventeen, thin lines of worry dug into the skin around her lips. She averted her gaze.

"What can I do? You're only fourteen. How are you going to work? What are you going to do for money? We only have a small flat . . ." Her voice trailed off.

My face crumpled. "Please, Natalie, please let me stay. I'll do anything."

"Your father's holding on, Tosca," Kevin interrupted. "What should I tell him?"

"Fuck off, Kevin," said Natalie curtly. "Tell him he can wait."

Kevin staggered back exaggeratedly. "Whoa, sorry!" He glared at me. "Do you want your family to be kicked out of the country? Why don't you stop being so selfish?"

"Selfish?" I cried.

I felt Natalie stiffen. "Tosca," she said hesitantly. "Maybe he's right."

"It's just because he bought you a flat," I said spitefully.

"What are you talking about, you little twit?" Kevin said with a nasty edge to his voice. "What's that got to do with deportation?"

Fear rippled through me. "Fuck everyone!" I cried. "But you'd better tell him I'm not coming back if he's going to hit me."

The ride back to London passed in a blur, and I sat miserably on the floor of the tube on my way home, hugging the blue and green plaid blanket I'd stolen from the coach. At the front door of our flat, I pressed the doorbell with a show of bravado, but inside I cowered, terrified.

Instead of hitting me or locking me up, my parents sent me to a psychiatrist. The doctor's office smelled like stale flowery perfume. He sat in his armchair and sucked on a shiny wooden pipe, nodding at me as I sat at the edge of the couch, tapping my foot to annoy him. He was dressed in a double-breasted brown suit, with gold cufflinks and shiny black lace-up shoes.

"What's the matter?" he asked in a thin baritone.

"I don't fucking want to be here," I said bitterly.

He scribbled something on the pad on his lap, the smoke from his pipe whirling in the air in a dense stinking cloud. Then his head rose and he met my eyes. I stared back, not looking away even after the corners of his lips turned downward and his eyes narrowed. He was trying to freak me out, I gloated inwardly. I wasn't going to give in one inch. I might have to be here, but I didn't have to *cooperate*.

"You're not very happy," he stated drily.

"Top marks," I laughed furiously, my head thrown back. "I'm fucking thrilled. Can't you tell?"

He stared at me, I stared back. Finally, he glanced at his wristwatch, put down his pipe, and showed me the door. Afterward, he called my parents and recommended that I see him three times a week.

"He's crazy," my mother snorted. "How much does he think we're willing to pay for this?" She pressed her freshly applied lipstick with a napkin and shut the case with a loud snap. "Let's send her somewhere else."

"What's the point?" griped my father.

"We have to do something," my mother retorted. "She's breaking all the dishes."

The second psychiatrist was chubby and pink, and after I was seated across from his desk, he handed me a glass of lime cordial.

"How do you feel about having the abortion?" he asked.

A fly landed on his arm and sat there, transfixed at a loose piece of thread in his jacket. The psychiatrist flapped it away and pulled down the cuffs of his sleeves, like he was self-conscious about his weight. He licked his finger with a quick movement before turning the next page of the pad.

I blinked back sudden tears. "I hated it."

"I can imagine it must have been quite a trial for you, being so young." He smiled sympathetically. "Do you feel like your parents care for you?"

"They hate me," I blurted. "All they ever do is punish me for everything. It's not my fault!"

"Why don't you tell me about it?" he responded.

For the next hour, I sobbed and hiccupped through what my parents did to me, the fighting, the imprisonment, the way my father punched me in the stomach when I was pregnant, the cutting of my hair.

"There's nothing wrong with you," he said at last. "You seem very well-adjusted, considering what you've gone through. The problem seems to be with your parents. They seem to be having some"—he paused before continuing—"problems."

He cleared his throat and viewed me warmly with his hazel eyes. "Maybe you should try to leave home as soon as you can. It's legal when you're fifteen. All you need is your parents' permission." He tapped his pen against his cheek. "When's your birthday?"

"In a month," I answered.

"How do you feel about leaving in a month?"

"How does it feel?" I squeaked. I bit my lip, eyeing him anxiously. "What if they say no?"

"The alternative is to wait until you're sixteen. The only way your parents are allowed to get you back then is if you can't prove you can support yourself. Prove, mind you. So if that's what you have to do, make sure you have a job and are living somewhere halfway decent." He looked at his watch, then stood up. "I'm sorry, dear, but our session has come to an end." He scribbled on a bit of paper and handed it to me. "Here's the number of a youth service you can call to get help with finding a job and a place to live. Best of luck."

I beamed at him as he showed me to the door. "Thank you, thank you, thank you!"

The psychiatrist rested his palm on the doorknob for a moment. "Some people think it's important for families stay together. They rarely think about the consequences of that on an unhappy family. Read R. D. Laing. That'll teach you all you need to know about families. Good-bye, dear."

My mother flipped closed her magazine in the waiting room. "What did he say?" she asked, standing up.

"Nothing," I mumbled, hiding my glee.

At home, I watched my mother serving lamb, potatoes, and green beans to my father, then to one and another of my siblings. Her hair was streaked orange and teased back so that it lay like a porcupine on her head. Green and purple eye shadow ran in crooked strokes around her eyes, and her cheeks sparkled with gold and red glitter above a thick plum lip line. She looked crazy, like a clown.

My father scrutinized his silverware for signs of dirt and hurled his fork over Marilyn's head into the sink. "Get me another one," he ordered, and Rock came running with the replacement, face creased with anxiety. In his suit, my father seemed professional, trustworthy, someone who was intelligent and respectable. He didn't look like a thief or a liar, or someone who had changed our name six times. He didn't look like he'd lived anywhere but in this apartment, this country, all his life. He placed his fork in his left hand and a knife in his right, just like British people when they ate. A stranger never would have guessed my father was anything other than rich and distinguished, a proper little English businessman, even if he did throw silverware over his children's heads.

The psychiatrist was right. My parents were crazy.

After supper, I tripped after my father into the living room. "Dad, if you give me permission, I can leave home. It's legal."

"What are you talking about?" My father removed a cigarette from the pack in his breast pocket. I laughed to myself as he irately tapped the cigarette against the table. He refused to buy another case, so sure the gold one would turn up one day.

"It's true," I said. "The psychiatrist told me."

"Be that as it may," he said. His eyes slanted upward at the corners. As he got older the Asiatic strain in his Jewish roots became more pronounced. "You do not have my permission to leave," he answered after a series of blinks. "And do you know why?"

I edged out of the way as in a cold, measured voice he expounded on the rules according to Aaron Ring, whoever he was.

"You won't eat right. You won't go to sleep on time. You won't go to school. You won't associate with the right people. You'll . . ." A look of disinterest washed across his face. "The answer is no."

"I really hate you," I shouted.

"What did you say? You come with me." He twisted my ear and pulled me into his bedroom. With one hand propping me against the wall, he took out a gold pen from his inside pocket and leaned over my mother's vanity table where a pad of paper lay. He tore off the top sheet that read in her spidery scrawl, "Glue—lipstick—new compact—stockings—" and printed in neat capitals, "I hate you." He looked calmly at me. "What else did you say?"

"What are you writing it down for?" I asked, my voice quavering.

"Ha! What am I going to do? What do you think I'm going to do?" His lip curled in triumph. "This is for court. This is to be used in evidence against you. I'm going to make you a ward of the state. They'll put you in a detention center." He chuckled. "You think you have it bad? Just wait until you get there. They'll keep you locked up until you're eighteen." He threw his head back, his new crowns flashing from his mouth. "Cat got your tongue?"

That night I stewed in agitation. In a cold fury, I ripped a sheet from my school binder. I drew fourteen squares with a ruler, angling the paper sideways to draw four more. Fifty-six altogether. One square for every week before I could leave home. In the last square lay my birthday, when I could get away from them forever. The minute I was sixteen, I was gone. There was no way they would ever get me back.

CHAPTER TEN

OFF THE TIGHTROPE

never believed in psychiatrists in the first place," said my father. "All they ever do is blame the parents."

"Yeah," my mother agreed, picking up a magazine from the coffee table. "They're just a bunch of quacks."

"Yeah, right," I muttered sarcastically under my breath as I headed toward Kirk's room.

"Hey, Kirk," I said casually. "Can I come with you to meet Toby tomorrow?" Toby had grinned that he was going to meet Kirk at Hyde Park, instead of going to school.

Kirk jolted. "How did you know?" he stammered.

"Toby told me." I swallowed. "Don't worry, I won't hang around."

He glanced sideways, realizing the trap. "Okay," he said reluctantly. "But you have to come back to meet me when I say."

Kirk told my mother we were going for a walk after school so we wouldn't be back until suppertime. On the way out, we dumped our schoolbooks in the umbrella stand in the lobby.

Frost crunched underneath our feet as we walked up the

ramp to Park Lane. Toby leaned against a lamppost outside the gates of Speakers' Corner with his hands deep in his black leather coat. He touched my brother shyly. They grinned like idiots at each other.

"'Bye," I called cheerfully, and strode down the ramp back toward the subway. A row of telephones stood by the wall in the station and I walked quickly, digging for the number in my pocket. I picked up the receiver and dialed, the phone slipping in my sweaty hand.

"Hello," answered a man. "Youth Help Service."

"Can you help me?" I said nervously.

"Are you in trouble?" he replied quickly.

I paused. "Not exactly. I just . . . uh . . . need to find out about a place to stay and . . . um . . . a job."

"Of course," he said. "Why don't you come down and we'll give you addresses of places you can try. The YWCA might be a good place to start if you need a place quickly. We have a bulletin board, too, with jobs posted. We're open 'til five."

"Great." I let out my breath. I moved to put down the phone.

"Wait a minute." He laughed. "Don't you need the address?"

I giggled. "Oh, yeah."

A man with long blond hair and deep blue eyes behind rimless glasses sat behind the desk in a small office at the top of a narrow staircase a couple of blocks from Paddington Station. Behind him on the wall was pasted a poster of children with gaunt faces: Save the Children. A bulletin board lay to the left, covered in notices: Jobs, Housing, Information, Pregnancy Services, Legal Aid, and Squatters Rights.

"Did you just ring?" the man asked, leaning forward to shake my hand. "My name's Richard."

I nodded. "Tosca."

"That's a pretty name." He came around the desk and indicated a folding chair against the wall. "Make yourself comfortable. How can I help you?"

My mouth felt dry. "You said I could find a place to live?"

"Yes. Where are you staying right now?"

"With my parents. I can't leave until I'm sixteen." I bit my lip. "In about nine months."

"Well, take a look at the board now to see what kind of places might be available, and when you're ready, you can come back and find something. Right?" He stood aside so I could look at the board. "Maybe write down some of the hostel addresses. And take a look at the jobs, yeah?"

When I arrived back at Marble Arch tube station, with the notes I'd taken jammed into my pocket, Kirk looked flushed and didn't notice how elated I was. On Marylebone Road, I skipped before him toward home, feeling heady and light, right into a crowd of people thronging outside our building. Flashbulbs exploded and shouts broke out as a resident came through the revolving doors.

"False alarm," a man grunted.

"What's going on?" I asked him.

His face lit up. "Here are the kids!" he said. He waved a

pad of paper in my face. "What did your father do?" The men swarmed toward us.

I jumped back. "Uh—"

"Keep quiet," Kirk warned me tensely.

The doorman shouted at the top of the stairs that if they didn't go away, he'd ring the police.

"Go on," called out a voice. "They're right upstairs."

Kirk grasped my arm and yanked me up the stairs. Outside the elevator on our floor, two policemen stood stiffly in the hallway, guarding our front door. One of them blocked Kirk as he tried to pass.

"Where do you think you're going, young man?" he asked sternly.

"This is my house!" he said angrily. "Let me through."

"Hey!" I shouted. "Let go of him!"

The policeman's partner grinned. "What do you say? Should we let the little buggers in?"

But Kirk had already jerked free and keyed open the front door. I pushed inside after him.

A policeman poked his head inside the door behind us. "Come, Mr. Rung, we don't have all day."

"I have to go." In the hallway, my father leaned toward my mother. "Joe or Frank will be in touch." Without another word, he stood between the two officers and was led away.

"Who's Joe?" I asked.

My mother tsked loudly. "What are you all standing here for? Don't you have anything better to do?" She glared at us.

"And don't let me catch any of you talking about this. You'll only get Dad into more trouble." She turned on her heel and disappeared into her bedroom. The clicking of the lock reverberated down the hallway.

"What do you think he did?" Fig whispered.

"I don't know," Kirk answered, frowning darkly. "Maybe we shouldn't talk about it. You heard what Mom said."

"Bloody hell!" I said. "We have a right to know what's going on."

Rock turned to Fig. He looked scared. "I heard him tell Mom something went wrong."

"What did he say?" I asked sharply.

He shrugged. "I couldn't hear." His lips puckered. "Is Dad going to come back?"

"Where is he?" Marilyn cried. "Why did they take him away?"

"He'll be back soon," Kirk said calmly to reassure her. "Don't worry."

"How do you know he'll be back?" Fig asked angrily.

"Dad's a con man," I said tartly. "Don't you know anything?"

Kirk shoved me. "How dare you say that? What do you know?"

I shoved him back. "Why do you think our name changed all those times? Don't you think he was trying to fool people?"

"What are you talking about?" Fig bunched his fists combatively. "He never changed our name."

I snorted. "You can't be serious. Don't you remember? Sawyer, Walters, Rung, even Smith, for Christ's sake."

"I don't think we should be talking about this," said Kirk nervously.

"Why not?" I retorted caustically. "Don't you want to know who he really is?"

Kirk slammed his fist against the wall. "You're always causing trouble! Why can't you drop it! Don't you see you're upsetting everyone?"

"You sound just like Mom," I taunted.

Fig forced himself between us. "Stop it!" he yelled. "Dad's in trouble and all you can do is fight!"

Rock's voice broke. "Is he going to come back?"

No one said anything.

"They have no right taking him away," he cried.

The phone kept ringing. "Stop calling!" my mother shouted at reporters on the other end. "It's none of your business!"

"Mom," Kirk called through her bedroom door. "Why don't you just make something up? That'll make them stop calling."

"What do you know?" she yelled. There was a bang, as if she had thrown something. "Where the hell is the phone book? I'm going to sue those bastards."

Kirk blinked rapidly. "I'm only trying to help," he mumbled. He caught me standing in the hallway. "Go to the store. There's no food."

I raised my eyebrows. "Me? Why do I have to go?"

He kicked the wall. "Because I said so, that's why. I'm in charge now."

"Fuck off," I said, and punched him. Then I ran back into my room and propped a chair against the door so he couldn't get in.

The soft yellow halos of the streetlights lit the shadows on the street below. A police siren whirred in the distance, and across the road, a lone man slouched under a cap as he smoked a cigarette. I wondered where my father was. He hadn't looked so sure of himself, caught between the two policemen like that.

The next morning, the *Times* lay on the doormat as usual. My father's face stared at me from the front page beneath the caption, "Resident American Extradited on False Bankruptcy Charges." I gripped the paper and read:

> Aaron Rung, a.k.a. Ring, has been detained for questioning by Interpol regarding an allegedly fraudulent bankruptcy filing in the United States and criminal activities in Britain, the Bahamas, and Florida. Rung, the father of seven children, is charged with failing to present evidence necessary in the 1962 bankruptcy case of his allegedly Mafia-run stock brokerage firm. Over one hundred investors have filed complaints. His British company, Lion, Ltd., allegedly has been running a criminal investment scheme into Scotch whisky,

also suspected of Mafia connections. When agents inspected the warehouse address in Argyll listed in Lion, Ltd.'s records, they found it empty, with no trace of whisky ever having been there.

Mrs. Rung and their seven children in Britain refused to comment. Rung lived in Scotland for three years before moving to London more than a year ago. Previously, he lived in New York where the charges were originally made. He is suspected of living in several other locations under different aliases.

A former partner, Ralph McKenzie of Glasgow, commented that when he sold Rung his whisky marketing firm, he had no idea that Rung was wanted in the United States. "He is a fine man. I'm sure there have been no improprieties. No doubt, a simple misunderstanding that will be cleared up. I have every confidence in him."

It is unknown how long Rung will be out of the country. A spokesman for the Foreign Office commented, "It is usual for us to extradite foreign residents in cases such as this."

So that was it.

I shook with fear and rage.

Fig and Rock spooned cereal into their bowls as Marilyn stumbled through the doorway in her pajamas, rubbing her eyes.

"Where's Mom?" she asked.

"Eat your cereal," commanded Kirk, and he handed her a bowl.

I held up the paper. "Look at this," I demanded, pointing at the photograph. "Resident American Extradited on False Bankruptcy Charges." As I continued reading aloud their eyes bored into me.

A fly darted around the water faucets. One of the taps dripped languorously. Fig stared blankly at the writing on the cereal box. Rock kicked his leg against his chair. Open-mouthed, Marilyn looked uncomprehendingly at each of us.

Kirk narrowed his eyes at me, accusingly. "See what you've done?"

"What?" I exclaimed.

"Didn't Mom say we shouldn't discuss it? And there you go!" His eyes were small and piercing. "Can't you ever listen to what they tell you?"

"No, I can't! I think we should know!" I threw the paper down. "He's not so great after all, is he! Just a bloody thief!"

Rock stopped kicking the table. "What does bankruptcy mean?"

Kirk and I answered at the same time.

"Nothing," said Kirk.

"Stealing from people who trust you."

"Why would he want to do that?" asked Rock. "Why would he lie?"

Kirk pressed his lips together. "He didn't, stupid. Someone made it up." His voice rose. "Didn't you hear Mom saying it was a lie?"

"That's right," said Fig. "Don't listen to Tosca. She's just a troublemaker."

Rock's face twisted as he looked at me. "Why do you always have to say bad things about Dad?" he cried. "All you ever do is fight with him. Leave him alone!" He threw back his chair and ran out of the room.

Fig's eyes flashed above the Cheerios. His voice was taut. "Mom said we can't talk about it. She said he could get into more trouble."

I laughed angrily. "You really think that's true? What more trouble could he be in, you idiot?"

Kirk pointed at Marilyn, who was in tears. "See what you've done?"

My mother appeared around the door, looking disheveled. She still wore yesterday's outfit. "What's going on in here?" she said with a frown. Long black lines of mascara stained her cheeks, and her lashes lay crookedly from her eyelids.

"Nothing, Mom," said Fig, going to her side.

Her eyes hardened. "What have you got there?"

"Here, Mom," I said, handing her the newspaper. I felt sorry for her as I watched her reading it. Maybe it wasn't her fault. Maybe he'd been lying to her, too. But she had the paper above her head and was trying to rip it in half.

"The nerve!" she cried. "How dare they print this garbage!"

Kirk patted her sleeve. "It's okay, Mom. We didn't believe it anyway."

"Yeah, Mom," said Fig, glaring at me.

The phone rang. My mother grabbed it and shouted into the receiver, "What do you want?" Then her voice broke. "Oh my god, where are you?" She didn't notice that we were still there, hanging on to her words. "You are? Thank god!" She slumped against the chair and closed her eyes.

I slipped out and raced to my parents' bedroom. I picked up the phone and put it to my ear.

"Hello? Who's there?" said my mother's voice. "Get off the phone."

I held my breath.

"It must be the line," my father said. He sounded jubilant. "Frank and Joe fixed it. I can get out of here tomorrow."

"Really? You mean it?"

"Yes, yes, it's all over. *Finito.*"

"But how—" my mother asked quizzically.

"You know me, always able to get myself out of a jam." He chuckled. "I just threw them some moola."

My mother froze. "How much did you have to pay?"

"What does it matter? For god's sake, aren't you happy?"

"Of course I'm happy." But her voice was clipped, angry. "It's all over the papers. Everyone in the building will know."

"What the hell, we'll move!" he said jovially. "We'll get a new name. Where do you want to go this time?"

I stopped breathing. Move?

"I don't know." My mother sounded unconvinced. "What about your office?"

"Oh, that's easy," said my father. I could imagine him waving his hand in the air, as if he were talking about where to dry clean his suit. "What do you say to Australia? A lot of orders have been coming in from there. Is that far enough for you?"

"No need to be sarcastic." My mother stayed silent for a moment. Then she let out her breath in a hollow whistle. "When should I start packing?"

"In a couple of days. I should be back by then with the tickets."

I stared at the bathroom floor for a long time. Then I went into my room and threw my duffle bag on the bed. I packed everything into it—my clothes, my books, my records, and the autograph book from New York, the one thing I had brought from the only place that had ever felt like home. I checked under the mattress, pocketed the addresses I'd written down at the Youth Help Service, and counted my money. I had only ten shillings left since I'd run away to Glasgow.

My mother was clearing plates and the kids were drinking their milk in the kitchen as if everything were normal. The bed in my parents' room was still unmade, and clothes were scattered all over the room. I found her purse underneath the vanity table and snatched a handful of money.

The door slammed against the wall.

"Mom!" I spluttered.

"Why aren't you in the kitchen doing the dishes? I've been looking for you everywhere," she said. She noticed my hands. "What the hell are you doing? Who said you could go into my purse? Give me that!" She lunged over and tried to snatch the money.

"You can't touch me," I shouted. "I'm not going with you. I'm leaving. You can't make me go anywhere. I need this money. You owe it to me."

My mother's hot breath fell on my cheek. "What are you talking about?"

"I'm not moving! I'm never ever going to move again! You can't make me!"

Her eyes narrowed into black slits. "You just wait until Dad gets back. Boy, are you in for it this time." She pointed to the door with a trembling hand. "Now get into the kitchen and do the dishes like you're supposed to. I don't have time for this."

"Fuck the dishes!"

My mother spun around. "That's it! I've had enough of you!" Her nostrils flared.

My teeth chattered so much I could hardly speak. "That's the last fucking time you are going to threaten me."

My mother drew herself up so that she was almost as tall as me. "How dare you talk to me like that. Give me the phone. I'm going to call Dad right now. I'm going to have you locked up." Sweat riveted down the sides of her nose.

I glared at the black stains high on her forehead from the last dye job, the tiny balls of glue around her eyelids, her thin nose, the lipstick around her lips, her narrow chin. Then I shoved her aside and sped to my room.

She ran so close behind me, my back tingled with her fury. "That's it. Either you shut up or leave."

I turned around and laughed hysterically. "You're not telling me to leave. I'm telling you." I picked up my bag and made for the front door.

"Just you wait. You're going to get it," my mother screamed all the way back into her bedroom.

Kirk stood with the phone in the hallway, sobbing to Toby that he didn't know what to do.

"Why don't you leave?" I said, nudging him.

He shrugged me off. "Fuck off!"

"Fuck you, too," I said. "Wimp." The front door gave a satisfying ring as I slammed it shut behind me.

Outside the building, I turned right. I walked and walked, and kept on walking off the tightrope between truth and lies. I didn't care that I was about to become another closed chapter. I knew which world I wanted to live in, and it wasn't theirs.

I was going back to being Tosca Ring, the name I was born with, and there I was going to stay.

ACKNOWLEDGMENTS

For reading earlier versions of this book and giving me great encouragement, much gratitude to Marci Klane, Denise Douieb, Meena Nallainathan, Rachel Sutton, Susan Dunstan, Susan Jacobs, and Donna Levin. Thanks also to my writing students who continue to give me the opportunity to share the process of writing one's way to the truth.

Thank you to David Sweet for his fine proofreading and Gretchen Achilles for her elegant design in creating a beautiful physical home for my story. My thanks are also to writers who had the courage to tell their own challenging, unconventional stories and kept me company as I unraveled the threads of my own.

Although my siblings and I have chosen different paths to cope with the legacy of our childhood, I am grateful that we have each survived in our own way. I am proud that, in the process, many of us became educators, artists, writers, and composers.

MARGO PERIN is the contributing editor of *Only the Dead Can Kill: Stories from Jail* and *How I Learned to Cook & Other Writings on Complex Mother-Daughter Relationships* and the poet of San Francisco's permanent memorial *Spiral of Gratitude*. A nominee for the Pushcart Prize, she has been featured in numerous national and international media, including PEN's *Fightin' Words*, *The San Francisco Chronicle Sunday Magazine*, *O, The Oprah Magazine*, Mexico's *El Petit Journal*, Holland's *Psycologie*, *KRON 4 TV*, *NPR's Talk of the Nation*, and *KALW, KPFA*, and *WAMC*. Her awards include two San Francisco Arts Commission Cultural Equity Grants, a Creative Work Fund grant, and residencies at Hedgebrook and Norcroft. You can find her at www.margoperin.com.